THE DEEP THINGS OF GOD

Reflections of a Jackleg Preacher

Ronald L. Glenn

ISBN 0-9767146-3-9
Printed in the United States of America

Sigfam Media Group, LLC
P.O. Box 27
Wilberforce, OH 45384
http://www.sigfam.com

Acknowledgments

The author is especially grateful to Loretta Lawrence, Paul Gates, Bertha Roundtree, and Saundra Menefee for critically reading early drafts of this book, and to Loga Michelle Odom, Michelle Daniels, and Janie Glenn for their encouraging feedback and editorial assistance. I owe special thanks to Jason Glenn for his technical expertise and Reverend Samuel Harris, Jr. for his usual excellent job with the cover design, text layout and graphics.

Dedication

This book is dedicated to Mother and Daddy

Allie Mae Willis Glenn
and
Devurn Henry Glenn

They introduced me to God and continue to walk
humbly before God.

*H*owever, as it is written:

"No eye has seen,
no ear has heard,
no mind has conceived
what God has prepared for those who love him"--
but God has revealed it to us by his Spirit.
*The Spirit searches all things, even **the deep things of God.***

1 Corinthians 2:9-10

Contents

RACE

THEOLOGY

Preface

REFLECTIONS OF A JACKLEG PREACHER

For who among men knows the thoughts of a man except the man's spirit within him? In the same way no one knows the thoughts of God except the Spirit of God. We have not received the spirit of the world but the Spirit who is from God, that we may understand what God has freely given us. This is what we speak, not in words taught us by human wisdom but in words taught by the Spirit, expressing spiritual truths in spiritual words. (1 Corinthians 2:11-13).

Truthfulness requires that I admit that I am a jackleg preacher. Webster's Collegiate Thesaurus lists synonyms for the adjective jackleg -- *amateurish, dabbling, dilettante, dilettantish, dilettantist, unaccomplished, unfinished, ungifted, unskilled.* I don't know what dilettante and those other French-sounding words mean, but I admit to being amateurish, unaccomplished, unfinished and ungifted, and I like to dabble in biblical studies from time to time.

Years ago I dropped into seminary for a while and then dropped out before I lost all sense of the divine. I almost lost the credentials needed to write this book when I decided recently to return to seminary and finish the work that I began. I could no longer claim to be a jackleg with such a degree, but it seemed the right thing to do in this complex and morally obtuse world. However, the seminary lost the record of the three terms I attended and cannot produce a transcript of my work.

My momentary irritation was surpassed only by my profound sense of relief.

Some biblical scholars scoff at the notion that we *"ignorant and unlearned"* (Acts 4:13, KJV) people can contribute in a meaningful way to scholarly debates. This is all the more true of a self-proclaimed jackleg preacher whose admitted gaps in formal theological education make any conclusions reached immediately suspect. However, we jacklegs have the advantage that comes from ignorance of formal theology. My sense of the religious is informed by an unwavering belief in the efficacy, vitality and reality of the spiritual realm. God, for me, is not an intellectual construction or the "Ground of being" spoken of by existentialist Paul Tillich. I believe that Jesus is the divine Son of God, Savior of the world who took human form. He remained God while human, but voluntarily *"emptied himself"* of his divine attributes. He retained his divine character, but entrusted his divine abilities to the One whom he called God, the Father. He prayed to the Father when he needed these abilities, but he did not retain the power to summon them without the intervention of the Father and the Holy Spirit.

Imagine the creation of something from nothing-- mass, human beings and all that exists--by a Being who can simply say, *"Let there be light and there was light."(Genesis 1:3)*. Or imagine eternity. Our finite minds demand that things have to have a beginning and they have to have an end. These things are beyond the scope of ordinary intellect. These are *deep things of God.*

Some have read the works of scientists who are interested in questions of cosmology, the origin of the universe. These scientists, for the most part, don't believe in anything or anyone other than themselves and the power of the human mind. Yet, some scientists who don't believe in God found that they eventually ran into God in their quest for reality. They usually used another name, not God, but often found themselves using words like "creation," as they worked their way back to the nanosecond after the seminal moment that they call the "Big Bang." These scientists ran the computer and found that God was moving around in the hard drive. The computers blew a fuse--if they have fuses anymore--when they tried to contend with God. These are deep things that studies cannot explain to us. Yet, the scripture says the Holy Spirit will reveal them.

This is not a book about the "hard sayings" of Jesus or difficult texts. Numerous scholarly works have been written about them. Deep things, in fact, can usually be expressed in simple, direct statements. They are deep because of their import and impact, not their complex construction or phrasing. Many of the chapters in this book were originally presented in sermonic form and then transcribed and edited. They retain pacing and rhythms that point to that heritage.

This book is written for genuine people living in the real world. Countless numbers of ordinary people look to the Bible as a source of inspiration and guidance during times of struggle and stress in their lives. There are many times when they need to consider *the deep things of God*. When my real estate agent's twelve year old son died of an asthma attack on a smoky Sunday afternoon in Pittsburgh, he was rudely shoved into deep, faith-shaking waters. He demanded that I, his pastor, talk to him about *the deep things of God*. I can still hear his trembling voice, "Time out for trivial pursuits, Pastor. My son is dead." When the plane carrying the lovely, young, intelligent fiancée of my friend and colleague crashed on a clear cloudless night in September, he was compelled to consider *deep things*.

The Christian husband of a Christian wife called me late one night and told me that if I didn't come over right away he would kill her. I knew him. He was serious. I knew her, too. She could be a real pain sometimes, but she didn't deserve to die like that. I got dressed and drove off into the night. My own personal domestic tranquility was shattered by this imminent, urgent confrontation with *the deep things*. When a single mother returned from a meeting with the judge and the confessed pervert who had sodomized her four-year-old son, she demanded that I talk about *deep things* because the perpetrator had been released to his house four blocks from her home.

Some argue that only well-trained and educated, reverend doctors, who have earned the master of divinity degree, are qualified to write about the deep things. We, the ordinary people, living in the real world must confront life's many trials, reach our own understanding, and achieve our own sense of peace. Therefore, we think about, worry about, and pray about the deep things every day. Besides, I have little confidence in this point of view when I consider the fact that the reverend doctors can't seem to agree on very many points of theology, even within the same denomination. So, with the naive enthusiasm and arrogance of a card-carrying jackleg preacher, I have written about *the deep things of God*.

MIRACLES

Miracles are events that seem to occur outside of the ordinary rules that govern the universe as it is understood and perceived by human beings. They differ from other extraordinary events in that they are attributed to the realm of the divine. Many people consider miracles to be beyond human understanding and part of the deep unfathomable works of God.

Not all things that are miraculous are supernatural. The next six chapters examine some things that are truly miraculous yet accessible if we use a fresh perspective about how God works.

MIRACLES

Chapter 1

THE DEEP THINGS OF GOD

"Then the Lord said to Joshua, 'See, I have delivered Jericho into your hands, along with its king and its fighting men'." *(Joshua 6:2).*

There was a time in the history of the people of God when they faced seemingly insurmountable challenges. You know the story of the great city called Jericho that had walls so thick and so high that they appeared to reach the sky. Yet, God told Joshua, *"I have delivered Jericho into your hands."(Joshua 6:2).* This band of Hebrew nomads started marching around the great wall. Imagine how they must have looked to the soldiers standing on the wall who observed a group of strange people marching in an orderly pattern around the wall. When a Jericho soldier looked over the wall and reported what he saw, the king must have thought he was crazy. The conversation might have gone like this: "You mean to say that they don't have any weapons pointed at us? They don't have a massive army ready to storm the gates? No, they're just marching. This is foolishness."

The king could not have known that the God who designed the universe designed fundamental particles of matter called atoms and molecules that are so small that the eye cannot see them. All matter vibrates with a certain natural frequency with vibrations so fast that the ear cannot hear them. If a sound is produced that matches a natural frequency, it reinforces the natural vibration and causes it to grow. Scientists call this phenomenon resonance. Ella Fitzgerald could sing a note so pure that it matched the natural frequency of a glass, causing it to shatter. Soldiers know not to march in step across a bridge because the vibrations from the marching might hit the natural frequency of the bridge causing resonance and the collapse of the bridge.

I cannot prove that the Jericho walls fell because of physical phenomena like resonance. I am sure, though, that the miracle of Jericho was not necessarily supernatural. It was, nevertheless, the miraculous result of obedience to the urgings of the Holy Spirit who revealed *the deep things of God*. Joshua was not a physicist. He did not know about molecules and the energy associated with their vibrations. The directives must have sounded strange: march in step, shout in a rhythm, and blow the trumpets when God tells you to do so. Obedience to the strange orders coming from God and faith that God's prophetic promise was true led to the famous result--the walls came tumbling down.

We have, seemingly, insurmountable walls today. This is a time of great turmoil and confusion in our society and in the church. Violence is rampant and crimes are pervasive. Academic studies proclaim that some children are innately inferior and a waste of society's resources. The recent presidential election in the United States clearly signals changes of the national mood and the will to address the problems of our society, but it is merely a beginning. Any reasonable analysis of the situation in the world would lead us to conclude that we are still in trouble.

Our historic response to trouble has been to seek political solutions that have not worked. Educational programs have generated weak, compromising platitudes that confuse our young people, leading to indecision and immorality. We cannot solve these problems because we are trying to use human wisdom. Yet Paul tells us that, *"No eye has seen, no ear has heard, no mind has conceived what God has prepared for those who love him". (1 Corinthians 2:9).* Why can't we conceive what God has planned for us? The answer to this question is clearly stated but we often ignore it. God has great things in mind for *those who love God.*

There was a time in the history of the people of God when God caused the writer to use a metaphor to describe the condition of the people that made them unable to understand *the deep things of God.* Ezekiel revealed that *"He said unto me, son of man, these bones are the whole of Israel. Behold they say our bones are dried and our hope is lost and we are cut off on our part." (Ezekiel 37:11).* I would not attempt to preach the classic "dry bones" sermon because I have neither the skill nor the nerve to try. I could never connect the bones like the great preachers of old, but I humbly and boldly suggest that this divine metaphor applies once again to some people in our society today from whom hope has evaporated, leaving behind the modern-day rubble of dry bones.

Ezekiel was speaking to a divided, discouraged, exiled, oppressed and hopeless nation. There appeared to be no solution; there appeared to be no way out. Is there a way out for God's people today?

Let us consider how Ezekiel pondered *the deep things of God* and unveiled his findings to the people. The Spirit of God spoke to Ezekiel and told him what to do. Examine what the Spirit did not tell Ezekiel. The Spirit did not tell Ezekiel to depend on the government. The Spirit did not tell Ezekiel to gather a great army. The Spirit did not tell Ezekiel to abandon hope. What deep thing did the Spirit tell Ezekiel? What esoteric, intellectual, brave, or powerful thing was Ezekiel to do? Pay careful attention to the Bible's revelation of this great mystery. *"Therefore prophesy and say to them: 'This is what the Sovereign Lord says: O my people, I am going to open your graves and bring you up from them; I will bring you back to the land of Israel." (Ezekiel 37:12).* This deep secret thing from the mind of God was to preach to the people who were buried. Preach to the people who were covered or overwhelmed by the circumstances of life. Preach to the people who were oppressed, and tell them that God said that their graves would be opened and then tell them, *"I will put my Spirit in you and you will live, and I will settle you in your own land. Then you will know that I the Lord have spoken, and I have done it, declares the Lord." (Ezekiel 37:14).*

Many of us are in exile from our past in a strange land politically and in a dry land spiritually. But, God has promised restoration. God has promised to open our graves and remove our grave clothes. The time for the shallow cover-up is over. The time for the superficial is over. It is time now to search for and listen to *the deep things of God.*

These passages from the books of *Joshua* and *Ezekiel* demonstrate that *the deep things of God* come from God's Holy Spirit dwelling in those who love God. The walls are great but, if we let the Holy Spirit lead us they can be brought down. Bones are dry but, if we let the Holy Spirit reside in us, they can rise up from their graves invigorated. We can't solve problems when we try to apply our humanness with all of its limitations. God gave the answers in the scripture by saying that God has revealed them unto us through the Spirit who searches all things, *even the deep things of God.*

Chapter 2

GOD-MAN WALKING

During the fourth watch of the night Jesus went out to them, walking on the lake. (Matthew 14:25).

What comes to mind when you think about God walking? Do you imagine long legs with two great big feet slowly placed one in front of the other? What would it sound like? Do the feet of God shuffle, or move quickly and briskly through the garden? All we know for sure is that Adam and Eve *heard the sound of the LORD God as he was walking in the garden in the cool of the day. (Genesis 3:8)*. Modern thinkers would laugh at this imagery as they deride us for our literalist thinking. They would argue that this is merely a poetic way of expressing the idea that God's presence moves in a way that we humans can sense and feel.

Many would bring the same poetic sensibilities to the story of Jesus, the God-man, walking on water. Issues like this cause me the greatest frustration about my jackleg status. I wish that I could read the Hebrew books that are in my library to impress visitors and make them think that I studied Hebrew for more than a month. A study of the word that is translated "walking," might reveal its deeper meaning and allow me to form an accurate mental picture of God's stroll in the garden. Left to my own devices, I will try to go through a less rigorous analytical process and see where it leads.

Think about this work we have chosen, whether ministers or lay persons, who have claimed Jesus as our Savior. List the requirements for this work. We have to be properly educated and trained. We need to have a calling, the will, and a sense of purpose. We often forget one of the most important things; we must be able to walk on water. I'm not sure why we don't usually see this listed in the job description. We need to be reminded from time to time of this necessary ability, especially those of us who have been in ministerial service for a while. When I entered the ministry, it was no problem for me, because I didn't have enough sense to know that I couldn't walk on water. I just fixed my eyes directly on Jesus and walked.

If you listen to those who are starting in the ministry, you will find that in those first moments, right after Jesus has touched them, and right after the call, they are so filled with faith and determination that walking on water is a simple matter to them. They do it without thinking about it. They just jump out of the boat and walk. If we don't practice and refine our walk, our struggles, challenges and failures can cause us to lose the faith that is necessary to retain this ability.

Jesus had just finished feeding thousands of followers with just a little bit of starting material when he sent his disciples over to the other side while he spent some time with friends. You know that Jesus always had a plan. He did not do things that did not make sense. Maybe the disciples thought he went to hire another boat. Maybe they thought that he was going to wait there until they got back. I'm not really sure, because the scripture doesn't tell us what he told them. He went up to the mountain privately to pray. But, this is no accident. Remember, this is Jesus.

The disciples' boat was out in the middle of the sea being tossed by the waves because the wind was strong. Imagine yourself out in the middle of that storm when you looked up and saw a figure that seemed to be walking toward you. You would probably think, "Maybe it's the fog, the storm; or maybe it's a ghost." They were afraid. Jesus said, *"Take courage. It is I. Don't be afraid." (Matthew 14:27).*

He knew that the disciples had seen him perform many miracles. But, there were at least 40 people who were pretenders to the real throne of God, who had from time to time led people off to follow them as they claimed to be the Messiah. There had been others who, through trickery, caused miracles to appear to be performed. Jesus' disciples were very impressed with Jesus, but they still did not understand the fact that Jesus is the unique Son of God who has a special purpose for us to carry out. The disciples needed to know for themselves the power of God. They could not be true followers of Jesus by sitting on the sideline watching the show.

Jesus knew his disciples and he knew Peter in particular. He was impetuous. He was not going to think things through clearly. He got excited in those initial moments when he saw Jesus walking. Jesus knew Simon Peter would say, *"Lord, if it's you, tell me to come to you on the water."(Matthew 14:28).* Peter probably was saying *"if it is really you, then..."* This "if...then" construction is familiar. Where have we seen it before? The devil said to a tired, hungry Jesus in the wilderness *"if...then." (Luke 4:1-12).* Now, a disciple is using that same construction to coax Jesus into revealing who he is. Jesus proved who he was. Peter walked on water for a while. He eventually sank, but he did not sink because the power of God failed. He sank because of the conflict in his own mind. I can imagine that he thought, "I'm doing what Jesus did and I am doing what Jesus called me to do. But, it does not make sense!"

This ordeal was important for Peter because he needed to know what he could do with the power of God. He wasn't going to be able to stand and watch Jesus. He needed to participate; so he jumped out of the boat and started to "walk." What an experience that must have been, walking on water in the middle of the stormy sea. That must have been exciting. More than exciting, that must have been exhilarating.

Then Peter became aware of the storm around him. Fear set in as he was walking on water while looking at Jesus. The storms of life have a way of making us forget about the miracles that we have seen. There's something about storm clouds that can make your memory get short, so that you forget the time that God brought you through. There's something about storms that can shake faith to its very foundation.

When you realize that you're standing on water, you think about Physics 101 which told you that in order for a person to stand in a particular place, there must be a balance between the force that is pulling down and the force that is holding him up. Someone standing on water in the middle of a storm realizes from experience that there is no force in that water that can hold him up.

Peter's problem was not the fact as some would suggest, that he took his eyes momentarily off of Jesus. It is true he saw the storm, and perhaps he glanced away. The thing that got Peter in trouble was that he allowed experience and history to come into his mind and take the place of faith. His experience as a fisherman told him that if he jumped out of his sturdy boat, he would sink. He knew from experience, long before Newton articulated his laws, that there was no counter force to hold him up.

The power of experience was so great that Peter began to sink. When you give in to the storm, you begin to lose even the things that you knew how to do. Peter began to sink even though he was an experienced swimmer. He forgot he knew how to swim and cried out, *"O Lord save me."* This experienced swimmer had the ability to save himself but Jesus had to stretch forth his hand to keep him from sinking. He chided him, *"You of little faith...Why did you doubt?"(Matthew 14:31).*

When they were coming back to the boat, the wind ceased and they worshiped him saying, *"Truly you are the Son of God." (Matthew 14:32).* And that was Jesus' point; that's what he was trying to show them. One day he was not going to be with them physically. He wouldn't be there to turn a few loaves of bread and a few fish into enough food to feed multitudes; the disciples would have to do it. He would not be there to lay hands on the sick and heal, or to say to the disabled, *"Get up and walk." (Luke 5:22).* The disciples needed to know for themselves that no matter what storms or forms of persecution were around them, they could walk on water.

The critical Bible reader seems to have three options when analyzing this story. Case one says that it simply didn't happen. This was an invention of the early church designed to impress new or wavering believers about the power of Jesus so that their faith could be strengthened. The second option says that indeed the story is literally true. That is, Jesus suspended the laws of gravity or changed physical properties such as density, and walked on the water. The third option, like the second, says that the story is absolutely, literally true. However, it suggests an alternative literal explanation of the events.

I didn't realize that there was a third option until I had been in the ministry over twenty-five years and had returned to seminary to take a series of courses on the

Gospels (*Matthew, Mark, Luke* and *John*). The professor suggested during our study of the *Gospel of John* that there was a device that could be used to remember the miracles of Jesus that were given as signs that he is the Messiah. This was referred to as "THE SIGN"--<u>T</u>urning water into wine, <u>H</u>ealing the nobleman <u>E</u>nabling the lame man. <u>S</u>atisfying the five thousand, <u>I</u>tinerating the water, <u>G</u>iving sight to the blind, <u>N</u>otifying Lazarus. The "I" stood for "itinerating the water." This choice of words, driven by the need to complete the acrostic and the lack of a "w" for walking, stimulated my thinking about the heretical scenario that follows.

Consider the common elements of this story given by the two gospel witnesses who wrote about it: The wind was contrary; Jesus looked as if he would pass them by; Peter could "walk" as long as he looked at Jesus and did exactly what he was doing; when he broke his concentration, he began to sink. If Jesus walked on water as it is usually translated, the laws of nature must have been temporarily suspended. The laws of physics demand that a person who is walking without sinking must have an upward force that balances his weight so that the net acceleration in the downward direction is zero. The upward push of the water is not usually enough to accomplish this. But, if the "I" in the acrostic reflects the correct sense of what Jesus did, then the water working with some other natural elements, might have done the job required by the laws of physics.

In my church denomination I am called an Itinerant Elder. That means that I am an elder who can be given an appointment by the bishop to travel. Saying that Jesus itinerated the water meant that Jesus "traveled" through the water outside of a boat. A few years ago a story was published about a sailor who traveled on the water for several days without a boat. He was not floating. He used a scooping motion to catch the wind in his coat and travel along the water. He would repeatedly scoop and travel, hour after hour. He did not have a lot of control with this motion. Steering was not easy. All of his energy must have been directed toward the scooping motion necessary for itineration. The uncertainty and imprecise control of the walking motion that led to the sense that Jesus might *"pass by them,"(Mark 6:48)*, coupled with the strong wind and the need for Peter to duplicate exactly the actions of Jesus through rapt focus and attention, are all consistent with this possible model.

It is here that the most conservative preacher-theologians get irritated and impatient with me. They are sure that I am not only a jackleg, but also a heretic because I appear to deny the complete supernatural ability of Jesus to suspend the laws of nature, defy gravity and mysteriously walk on water. Their accusation is misguided, however. Jesus' actions were clearly miraculous. But, they were not necessarily supernatural. The supernatural ability to defy any of the laws of nature is resident in the God-Head in general and the God-Man in particular. It was, however, only summoned by Jesus when absolutely necessary (such as when he called Lazarus forth from the dead). Part of his divine mission was to demonstrate that it is possible for human beings to trust God so completely that the Holy Spirit can empower them to respond to the call of God in their lives. Furthermore, the same Holy Spirit would give them the knowledge to do *"even greater things"* within the bounds of natural laws. *(John 14:12)*.

We modern-day disciples are still required to walk on water. We were called by Jesus to our journey. He demonstrated who he is. He demonstrated his power by calling us to walk. We do walk sometimes. But, every

now and then we feel ourselves begin to sink and we
have to cry out *"Lord, save me!"* *(Matthew 14:30).* When
we understand the key to walking on water, there are no
problems that we cannot solve. Jesus Christ, our Lord,
our Savior, died for us and rose again. Therefore, we
have the power.

Chapter 3

AFTER THE HEALING

Then Peter said, "Silver or gold I do not have, but what I have I give you. In the name of Jesus Christ of Nazareth, walk." Taking him by the right hand, he helped him up, and instantly the man's feet and ankles became strong. He jumped to his feet and began to walk. Then he went with them into the temple courts, walking and jumping, and praising God. (Acts 3:6-8).

This is a very well-known scripture about a disabled man who had a special encounter with the divine. Two apostles, Peter and John, were going to the temple, a place of worship and sacrifice. They were able to go there because they were apostles and because they were men who met all the criteria given in *Deuteronomy* and other places in the *Hebrew Scripture* that placed restrictions on who was able to go into the temple and serve God.

Peter and John were going into the temple in the afternoon at the time of prayer. A man was there who was crippled from birth. He had to depend on somebody to carry him to the gate where worshipers entered into the temple court. He had come there long enough to know where the good begging spots were. His life's circumstance had forced him to do the research and this man probably had the equivalent of a B. S. degree in strategic planning as a result of his condition. He had concluded that the choice spot was near the entrance where the people who were feeling holy and righteous and close to God would have to pass by. He was placed outside the door, outside the gate, outside the entrance, because he was a defective, deformed, imperfect human being who was forbidden by law from going inside.

That day he had on his usual face expecting that this was going to be a pretty good begging day. When he saw Peter and John about to enter, he asked them for money. Peter and John looked straight at him and said, *"Look at us."* That's a very rich statement because it would have been human nature to look away from him. There's something about a direct gaze that makes people a little uncomfortable. They may just toss a coin at him and keep on going into the temple where they could still feel holy, righteous, and pure. He had learned over the years that if he expected to get something from folks, he should always look down. He knew not to look them in the eyes, because they might think that he was insolent and arrogant. He got used to looking down.

The man looked at them with a sense of expectancy. He was sure that his begging strategy was working that day. He was in the right position. He had the right look of desperation and hopelessness; it was a pitiful look designed to elicit the warmest response.

Then they dropped the bombshell. They did not have what he wanted. They did not have any silver or gold. The man had to be very puzzled and confused by this time. What else is there, if they don't have any money? Isn't that what it's all about? Isn't that what everybody wants and needs? He had been in this condition since he was born. He had been unable to go into the house of God and worship. The only thing that gave him some relief was a little money in his cup to buy the goods and services that he needed.

Instead of money they gave him a name. *"In the name of Jesus of Nazareth, walk." (Acts 3:6).* Society often says something to lame men that sounds similar, but is not quite the same. "For Christ's sake, why don't you get up and do something for yourself?"   This question is hurled like a derisive epithet at the man who is down.

Peter didn't just tell him to get up; he took him by the right hand.   Peter understood that somebody who had been in a helpless, hopeless situation all his life needed help from his brothers and his sisters to deal with the uncertainty of his new status. He began slowly to get up for the first time in his life, holding on tightly to Peter's hand, with John on the other side. Instantly, the man's feet and ankles became strong, and he jumped to his feet and began to walk.

After the healing, what did the man do? When he was finally able to walk, where did he go? He did not go running down to the dance hall. He didn't even rush home to see his family to show them that he could walk.

There were restrictions also on where one could sit. Special places were reserved for certain people. If you were of the right race and color, you could sit in one section. If you were of the right gender, you could go to another designated place. If you were of the wrong gender, you were barred from certain areas. Some people were completely excluded from entering the temple. That's the way it was in the house of worship during the time that this event with Peter and John took place. Not everybody could just walk into the temple and worship God. This man had been excluded from the temple, unable to go into the temple to make a sacrifice.

The first thing he did when God enabled the muscles of his thighs to work, was to go into the temple area where he could worship God. Some of you can't relate to this because you have been blessed and don't understand what it means to be disabled and ostracized and placed on the outside of society. You've never been in a situation where you had to look up at people who were looking down their noses at you.

Peter gave his hand to him and helped him up. Standing was still new to him. Walking was uncertain. So what did he do? He held on to his brothers who gave him the name that enabled him to stand. God gave him this gift, but didn't expect him to do it all by himself. He could hold on to those who were more experienced in this walk. After the healing, go into the place of worship, hold on to your brothers and sisters and praise God.

Chapter 4

FROM THE MUNDANE TO THE MIRACULOUS

"Here is a boy with five small barley loaves and two small fish, but how far will they go among so many?" Jesus said, "Have the people sit down." There was plenty of grass in that place, and the men sat down, about five thousand of them. Jesus then took the loaves, gave thanks, and distributed to those who were seated as much as they wanted. He did the same with the fish. (John 6:9-11).

The writers of the Synoptic Gospels often seem to be having a wonderful three-way conversation while the writer of the *Gospel According to John* seems content to go his own way. A notable exception is the story of Jesus feeding the multitudes. There are six accounts in the four gospels with differing details and numbers of people fed. All of the gospel writers recognize the pivotal significance of these mass feeding events in demonstrating the power of Jesus as the Christ.

Consider some common elements of the various accounts. The disciples told Jesus that the people were hungry and that he should send them away to get something to eat. Jesus told them not to send them away. Feed them. This command led to an incredulous response from the disciples. They argued that there was not enough food to satisfy so many. Jesus told the disciples to take inventory and see what they had. Jesus demonstrated many times to his disciples that they should consider what they had as a starting point in order to prepare for increase.

Jesus often taught and preached to crowds of people on the side of a mountain. Sometimes Jesus would sit down and get comfortable because he knew that they would be there for a long time. He did not have a good amplifying system, so he needed a place where the acoustics were good and even a soft voice could catch the wind as it traveled down the mountainside, cascading down to the valley.

The *Gospel of John* lists specific miracles that Jesus performed and characterizes them as the signs that he was the Messiah. Many people came to hear him preach because they had heard about the miracles. He knew that many of them had traveled a long way, so that they were tired and weary, yet willing to sit at the feet of the Master. He had great compassion for them.

We should always pay attention to what Jesus says and what he does with his disciples. Jesus asked a question to which he knew the answer as a test for his close disciples. They had seen the miracles. They should have known the answer. They should have known that Jesus could easily supply the food that they needed. He could supply all of their needs if necessary. He posed the question, *"Where are we going to get food for all of these people?"*

These gatherings seemed to have some similarities to the old-fashioned outdoor revival meetings where large crowds came from the surrounding towns to hear the charismatic traveling preacher who gained popularity by word-of-mouth. So, Jesus was sitting on the mountaintop, running a revival for all of his followers. There were some in the crowd who had just come for a show. Some may have thought that they needed a miracle in their lives and that they might get it up on the mountainside. It was in this setting that Jesus turned to his closest disciples and asked: *"Where shall we buy bread for these people to eat?" (John 6:5).*

Note that Jesus asked this question of his close disciples. If we apply this in today's terms, Jesus would be asking the Church, "What are we going to do for all of the people who have traveled a long way seeking me? They are weary, tired and hungry." He did not ask the crowd. He turned to his disciples. He turned to the ones who knew him. The disciples looked at him in amazement and were probably thinking "Do you know, Jesus, how much food it would take? Look at the crowd." *Philip answered him, "Eight months' wages would not buy enough bread for each one to have a bite!" (John 6:7).* The answer came from one of the close disciples who began to make excuses about how big the crowd was. This answer is significant because it came from one who knew Jesus and had seen him perform many miracles.

One disciple, Andrew, the brother of Simon Peter, spoke up. He suggested that they needed to do something educators, administrators and social services workers do. They took inventory. They looked around to find out if there was anybody who brought food with them. There are six accounts of this story in the Gospels and all four Gospels say that the disciples canvassed the crowd to take inventory. They asked brothers and sisters in the crowd whether they had any food. Imagine that they looked at one man and asked if he had any food. He shook his head to say no. They asked others who also said no. I can imagine them approaching a tall, six-foot burly man in the crowd who rolled his eyes at them and turned away. They kept on roaming through the crowd looking for food. Eventually, they went back to Jesus and reported. Andrew said, *"Here is a boy with five small barley loaves and two small fish,...(John 6:9).*

This little boy was probably sitting there minding his own business, guarding his lunch that Mama or Grandma had prepared for him. Let's speculate about how the scene may have unfolded. This was a boy who was nestled there among all of these grown folk who had come looking for a miracle. This little boy was sitting there with his brown paper bag with a greasy spot on it from the nicely fried fish he carried. His parents had probably given him his lunch just in case he became hungry and told him to sit quietly with his playmates while they watched for Jesus to perform one of his miracles. He held on tightly to his little fish and small loaves of bread.

Can you imagine the reaction of this little boy when the disciple came by and said, "Here is a boy with some food!"? The Bible does not tell us that the boy offered his food to the disciples. It simply says that the boy was sitting there and he had some food. He might have offered it. I probably would have if I was a small boy and a big man came along looking for food. I suspect that when the disciple said, *"Here is a boy with five small barley loaves and two small fish "*, he had already taken the boy's lunch bag to examine what was in it. The little boy, mindful that his parents had taught him to be respectful of adults, did not hesitate to give up his lunch. Jesus seized this opportunity to illustrate the child-like characteristics that he tried to instill in his disciples. He had said that only those who became as a little child could be saved. A child is trusting, a child loves, a child is dependent and as some modern liberal theologians have pointed out, a child is powerless. The child trustingly gave his food to the disciples when they requested it.

Jesus made the disciples organize the people by seating them in an ordered way. He was showing the disciples that it would be easier to solve a big problem if they took the chaotic and random presentation of the problem and structured it in such a way that they could see it clearly. Thousands of people scattered all over a mountainside would seem to be much more daunting, than the same people seated in organized groups.

The disciples were watching closely as Jesus lifted the bread and the fish toward heaven and prayed. *John* doesn't give us the content of that prayer. We can only imagine what Jesus said. We can suppose that he first gave thanks to God, the Father for his provision. He might have loudly proclaimed his gratitude for the food that was provided by this unselfish child. No one else showed any food in response to the disciples query. Thank God for the little child.

Then, the miracle happened. The disciples began to distribute the food to the waiting crowd. Hundreds, then thousands were fed and satisfied. Several baskets of food were left over. This miracle is cited by *John* as one of the signs that Jesus is the Christ. It is a very good sign. We need to be reminded, however, that not everything that is miraculous is supernatural. The Bible does not tell us how Jesus produced the food. What a miracle, to take molecules of fish and bread and create new molecules of fish and bread out of nothing! This would have been an easy task for Jesus to perform. After all, Jesus had performed many other miracles.

Consider the possibility that the actual miracle was greater than the production of new molecules of food. Jesus' miracle was certainly more than just an ego-driven stunt to impress people with his power. Jesus was always motivated by love and compassion. He was also determined to show the disciples that they could do everything that he was doing and would have the opportunity to do even *"greater things."* *(John 14:12)*. The key to this miracle was the prayer. Jesus always sought power from on high through prayer. The food materialized after the prayer. The miracle occurred because of prayer. How many members of the gathering were changed because of Jesus' prayer? How many of those who produced no food in response to the disciples' request were changed by the prayer. How many selfish hearts that had been hoarding and hiding food realized that Christ called them to share? Surely this child's grandmother wasn't the only one who prepared some food. No doubt many had brought a sandwich or snack to this deserted place to hear the master. Many of them came looking for a miracle not realizing that the greatest miracle would occur within their hearts.

Maybe Jesus transformed cold, egocentric, uncaring hearts of stone into compassionate, sharing, Christian hearts prepared to unite in a communal bond. Maybe adults, moved by a child's willingness to share, found the food, which was hidden when the disciples initially inquired. Jesus used the mundane quest for food to produce a miraculous transformation of human hearts.

Chapter 5

THE UNFINISHED MIRACLE

And he came to Bethsaida, and they brought a blind man unto him and asked him to touch him. He took the blind man by the hand and led him out of town. When he spit on his eyes, and put his hands on him, he asked him if he saw any thing. And he looked up and said, "I see men like trees walking." After that, he put his hands upon his eyes, and made him look up. He was restored and saw every man clearly. (Mark 8:22-25).

I find myself thinking a lot about miracles these days. It might be because the problems that we face seem so great that it's going to take a miracle to solve them. Ordinary means are not sufficient. Crime is so high that I'm not sure that regular solutions apply. It's going to take a miracle. Poverty is so deep and pervasive that traditional political and economic programs don't work. It's going to take a miracle. We read in the newspaper about tribal wars and genocide, brother against brother, sister against sister, and nation against nation. There is so much hatred and ill will in the world, that diplomacy is not going to solve the problems. It's going to take a miracle.

Those of us who have a special calling to ministry and service must know how to perform miracles. Some must stand behind a pulpit and preach about the miracle worker. Some of us have fingers that know how to make piano keys move to form beautiful sounds that honor

God. Some who are gifted with special voices can sing about how they made it through by the grace of God.

If we want to know how to perform miracles, we have to study the miracle worker. Jesus was a very effective miracle worker. Thousands were brought to him for cures from ailments that had troubled them for years. A man with a paralyzed hand was touched by Jesus and his hand was restored just as sound as the other. (*Mark 3:5*). The miracle was instant and complete. Jesus healed many other people and the healings were convincingly effective. (*Mark 3:10*). All things that Jesus did were done with authority. He even arose from his sleep in the middle of a storm, *rebuked the wind, and said to the waves, "Quiet! Be still!" The wind died down and it was completely calm. (Mark 4:39).*

When Jesus, the miracle worker, performed miracles, they were immediate and perfect, except for one strange case. In that particular circumstance a blind man was brought to Jesus so that Jesus might touch him. (*Mark 8:22-25*). People understood that if anything could be done for this poor blind man, Jesus could do it.

Jesus realized that in order for him to perform the miracle he had to move the man out of his immediate surroundings where some people had come to be entertained or to satisfy their curiosity about the popular preacher who was the dominant subject of local conversations. So, he took the man by the hand and led him out of town. There were some places where even Jesus could not do his best because there were too many distractions—too much cynicism, too many false interpretations of the gospel or simply intentional adulteration of his teachings. The scripture confirms that there were places where Jesus couldn't help some people due to skepticism or "lack of faith" which made it impossible to break through to them. (Mark 6:5-6).

Jesus wanted his disciples to know beyond any doubt that he was the Christ and they must deny themselves and follow him (Mark 8:22-38). They needed to guard against infusing the Pharisees' false teachings into the true gospel. His disciples began to realize that they were symbolically like the blind man. They saw a little bit, but didn't see the whole picture because self-interest, personal concerns, and outside distractions got in the way. That's why Jesus performed his only incomplete miracle.

When he had spit on his eyes and laid his hands on him, Jesus asked "Do you see anything?" He looked up and said, "I see people; they look like trees walking around." (Mark 8:23-24). This miracle left the observers, including the disciples, confused and perplexed. They didn't understand what they saw because they knew that Jesus was an expert in the miracle working profession. We need to put the entire scripture in its proper context to grasp an understanding of Jesus' "incomplete" miracle. Jesus' ultimate goal in performing the miracle in this fashion included teaching a lesson to his disciples as well as restoring the blind man's sight. He knew that his disciples needed absolute faith in God in order to continue the work that he started. It was very clear to Jesus from their behavior that the disciples still did not understand his mission. That is, the disciples had a blurred vision of Jesus' purpose on earth.

Just before the encounter with the blind man, Jesus and his disciples had gone across the river in a boat. The disciples forgot to take bread with them except for one loaf. *"Be careful"*, Jesus warned them. *"Watch out for the yeast of the Pharisees and that of Herod."* (Mark 8:15). Jesus was not talking about bread as the disciples assumed. He reminded them that they saw him perform many miracles including feeding thousands of people from a few loaves of bread. Jesus asked *"Do you have eyes but fail to see?* (Mark 8:18). They saw the miracles in the same way that they had seen theatrical performances. They did not understand the powerful works of Jesus.

As the story ended, Jesus touched the blind man one more time and *his eyes were opened, his sight was restored and he saw everything clearly. (Mark 8:25).* We Christians sometimes find that our vision is impaired. We may need to be touched one more time to get us through our incomplete miracles. When this happens we can also say *"I can see clearly"* everything that God expects me to do. Pray that God will touch us one more time so that our swelled heads can shrink a few sizes. Another touch will enable people who are unfinished miracles to stand humbly before the one who hung on the cross and declared for the entire world to hear, *"It is finished."* (John 19:30).

Chapter 6

DEEP WATER RELIGION

When he had finished speaking, he said to Simon, "Put out into deep water, and let down the nets for a catch." Simon answered, "Master, we've worked hard all night and haven't caught anything. But because you say so, I will let down the nets." When they had done so, they caught such a large number of fish that their nets began to break. So they signaled their partners in the other boat to come and help them, and they came and filled both boats so full that they began to sink. When Simon Peter saw this, he fell at Jesus' knees and said, "Go away from me, Lord; I am a sinful man!" For he and all his companions were astonished at the catch of fish they had taken, and so were James and John, the sons of Zebedee, Simon's partners. Then Jesus said to Simon, "Don't be afraid; from now on you will catch men." So they pulled their boats up on shore, left everything and followed him. (Luke 5:4-11).

Matthew, Mark and Luke all record the change in the lives of Peter, Andrew, James, and John from professional fishermen to the fishers of men that they became. Mark reports that James and John left their father and the hired men and followed Jesus. Likewise, Simon and Andrew immediately left their nets and followed him. (Mark 1:18). Luke, however, adds a small but significant detail. *When he had finished speaking, he said to Simon, "Put out into deep water, and let down the nets for a catch". Simon answered, "Master, we've worked hard all night and haven't caught anything. But because you say so, I will let down the nets." (Luke 5:4-5).*
Jesus had the audacity to tell these experienced fishermen how to catch fish. He was a carpenter who

learned his trade under the tutelage of his supposed father, Joseph. He was talking to experienced and seasoned fishermen. The bluntness of his directive obviously got on the nerves of Simon Peter and the others. Simon knew Jesus. He called him *"Master,"* yet, with undisguised reluctance, let down the nets. Many of us respond to the commands of Jesus in the same way. We act as if Jesus could not possibly have experienced what we are going through; he could not begin to know how to solve our problems. We tentatively say "Yes, Lord," as we cast our nets.

The disciples caught more fish than they could ever have imagined. *When Simon Peter saw this, he fell at Jesus' knees and said, "Go away from me, Lord; I am a sinful man!" For he and all his companions were astonished at the catch of fish they had taken, and so were James and John, the sons of Zebedee, Simon's partners. (Luke 5:8-10).* They were amazed that a jackleg fisherman could show them things about their craft that they had never understood. Simon recognized his own human sinfulness and incompleteness in the face of the power of Jesus. God has to reach us at the place of our apparent strength, in order to get our attention and direct our efforts toward doing the will of God.

Peter's declaration of his sinfulness is reminiscent of Isaiah's cry when he had a vision of the true God. *"Woe to me!" I cried. "I am ruined! For I am a man of unclean lips, and I live among a people of unclean lips, and my eyes have seen the King, the LORD Almighty." (Isaiah 6:5).* Isaiah had material wealth and status in society. He surely must have thought that he had it made. Yet, when he saw the majesty of God and beheld the glory of God, he realized that he was an unclean man living among unclean people. It was only then that he could submit to the will of God and declare, *"Here am I. Send me."* (*Isaiah 6:8*).

This was not the first encounter between Jesus and these four disciples. Andrew was the one who first met Jesus. *Andrew, Simon Peter's brother, was one of the two who heard what John had said and who followed Jesus. The first thing Andrew did was to find his brother Simon and tell him, "We have found the Messiah," (that is, the Christ). And he brought him to Jesus. Jesus looked at him and said, "You are Simon son of John. You will be called Cephas," (which, when translated, is Peter).* (*John 1:40-42*). Andrew found his biological brother Simon and brought him to Jesus. We who know the Lord must find our brothers and sisters and witness to them about the Savior. If each of us brought just one person a year to Jesus, our churches could be mega-churches. Andrew was not afraid to witness to his brother. He did not bring bad news. He did not bring gossip or skepticism. He brought the good news that he had found the Messiah. Andrew must have known that his outgoing brother would quickly push him into the background as he rose to a position of prominence. Yet, Andrew brought him to Jesus. Andrew was like his mentor, John the Baptist, who understood that he *"must decrease"* (*John 3:30, KJV*).

Jesus did not call Peter, Andrew, James and John to stop fishing. In fact, he recognized that their skills as fishermen prepared them for the work that they must do. Jesus was calling frustrated, irritated, burnt out fishermen to become effective in their new enterprise— fishing for converts to join the Kingdom of God. What were the attributes possessed by these *ignorant and unlearned* (*Acts 4:13, KJV*) fishermen? Fishermen know how to read the signs of the times. They know how to study the clouds, sense the winds and gauge the temperature to find the best conditions for catching the

different kinds of fish. Fishermen know what kind of
bait to use and how deep to set the lines and nets. They
have strong arms and broad shoulders that help them to
maneuver in rough waters. They can skillfully swim to
shore to try again after a shipwreck.

Jesus called these men to use the skills that God
had given them as they started this new enterprise. This
is an important lesson that I had to learn. When God
called me to the ministry, I was trained as a scientist and
working as a teacher and administrator. It took me many
years to understand that God did not want me to
abandon any of those skills and experiences. Rather,
God was calling me to use them all to proclaim the
Gospel in a special way. I used to teach science. Now I
teach people how to study the Bible and find for
themselves what God is saying to them and calling them
to do.   I once studied mathematical equations. I now
apply the same analytical processes to develop an
understanding of the marvelous Word of God. I used to
raise and spend millions of dollars as a university
administrator. Those same gifts of administration are
now applied to managing the church's resources in a
God-honoring way.

God is calling plumbers, electricians, restaurant
workers, doctors, and lawyers to apply their skills to the
glory of God. You can perform in any profession so that
people can see your good works and give honor to your
God in heaven. I knew a man who had an opportunity to
do his job in such a way that he could enrich himself and
avoid paying taxes. One of the men who knew about this
possibility chided the man for his refusal to earn his
money dishonestly. He said that there was no way that
any one would ever know. The man replied, "Yes, but I
will know and so will God."

After the crucifixion, the disciples decided to return to the familiar old ways. *Simon Peter, Thomas (called Didymus), Nathaniel from Cana in Galilee, the sons of Zebedee, and two other disciples were together. "I'm going out to fish," Simon Peter told them, and they said "We'll go with you." So they went out and got into the boat, but that night they caught nothing. (John 21:2-3).* Once again the disciples experienced failure and frustration. *Early in the morning, Jesus stood on the shore, but the disciples did not realize that it was Jesus. He called out to them, "Friends, haven't you any fish?" "No," they answered. He said, "Throw your net on the right side of the boat and you will find some." When they did, they were unable to haul the net in because of the large number of fish. (John 21:4-6).* Though the disciples didn't recognize Jesus, they responded to something in his voice and obeyed his command. The result this time, as in the first, was an abundant catch of fish, instead of failure.

When they landed, they saw a fire of burning coals. There were fish on it, and some bread. Jesus said to them, "Bring some of the fish you have just caught." Simon Peter climbed aboard and dragged the net ashore. It was full of large fish, 153, but even with so many the net was not torn. Jesus said to them, "Come and have breakfast." None of the disciples dared ask him, "Who are you?" They knew it was the Lord. Jesus came, took the bread and gave it to them, and did the same with the fish. (John 21:9-13). This meal is as important as the critical meal in the upper room where Jesus established the sacrament of Holy Communion. They both symbolize that after the resurrection, frustrated human effort is overcome by trusting in divine power.

In the first scriptural account, Jesus challenged his disciples to use their skills as fishermen to become fishers of men. They obeyed his command. Later, they became despondent after they thought that Jesus was no longer

with them. They decided to return to their familiar, life-
long trade. We, like the disciples, sometime revert to our
old ways and neglect our calling to win souls for Christ.
We feel that this is necessary in order to survive and
satisfy our physical needs. Jesus reminds us in this
second fishing encounter with his disciples that he
provides all of our needs. He had prepared breakfast for
them before they came ashore with their great catch of
fish. (*John 21:12-13*). He was telling us not to worry
about earthly matters of earning a living. If we listen to
his command and cast our nets on the right side of the
boat to win souls for him, the catch will be abundant.
We, then, will dine eternally on the feast prepared.

LOVE

God is love. This was the radical new idea brought into reality by Jesus through his powerful sacrificial life. It is hard for some to understand using our modern thought processes that God has an affectionate emotional connection to the divine creation. Gods were well-known as beings to be feared and appeased. They were not often thought to have benevolent feelings toward mortal human beings.

This love idea was so essential for Jesus that he made it the singular test of true discipleship. He also gave love as the explanation for the rashly irrational act of offering his own life for the salvation of sinful humans. The next two chapters draw our attention in a new way to "the greatest of these."

Chapter 7

TO HELL WITH THEM

The time came when the beggar died and the angels carried him to Abraham's side. The rich man also died and was buried. In hell, where he was in torment, he looked up and saw Abraham far away, with Lazarus by his side. (Luke 16:22-23).

*E*ternal torment in hell is such a pervasive and necessary part of the Christian psyche for some literal-minded fundamentalists that they transform God into an unrelenting, close-minded sadist who would eternally torture errant humans. The most amazing feat of Christian apologetics is the rationalization of the loving character of God with the God-ordained, pre-destined, unending torment and torture of hell. God's punishment --divinely imposed suffering--is not inconsistent with the character of a loving God. But God's punishment always has a redemptive purpose--redemption of a people or redemption of an individual. Punishment when redemption is impossible, such as in an eternal, endless tormenting hell, would be cruel and unusual. This is contrary to the loving nature of God.

William Barclay, in his book *Introducing the Bible*, lists four possible responses to those who offend us: "unlimited vengeance, precise retribution, conditional forgiveness, and absolute forgiveness." Never-ending torment in a burning hell would be a classic example of unlimited vengeance. This is not part of God's loving design. Barclay states it succinctly: "So the wheel has gone full circle; it began with unlimited vengeance, and it ends in Christ with unlimited forgiveness." At least one scripture supports this idea directly: *"I will humble*

David's descendents because of this, but not forever." (1 Kings 11:39).

One of my former students, who is now a minister, told me that he was sure that I am going to hell because I questioned whether the Bible really teaches unending torment as the intent of a loving God. I explained that I have no doubt about my Savior, Jesus Christ. I believe that he is my Lord and that he died for me. Nevertheless, he countered, "Jesus believed in a burning hell and you do not, then clearly you do not believe in Jesus." Arguments such as this have been used for years to make belief in a literal, burning hell a necessary condition for salvation.

A parable told by Jesus is often cited as proof that he believed in and taught a literal, eternal, tormenting hell. *The time came when the beggar died and the angels carried him to Abraham's side. The rich man also died and was buried. In hell, where he was in torment, he looked up and saw Abraham far away, with Lazarus by his side. (Luke 16:22-23).* This story follows immediately two parables designed to teach moral lessons to the disciples. Jesus used the traditional parabolic introduction to this story. Nevertheless, many insist that it is not a parable, but a literal re-telling of a story about a real rich man who is being tormented in hell. One commonly cited reason is the fact that the men in the parable had names. Other parables used generic terms such as *"a certain man."*

My former administrative assistant was taught to believe strongly in this kind of hell. She had been a Christian all of her life. Yet, when cancer brought death near, she began to believe that she was not saved. She was told that she could not be saved because she had never spoken in tongues to the satisfaction of the members of her church. She professed saving faith in Christ Jesus and faithfully paid her tithes and offerings.

She attended Bible study, but she still was not saved because the congregation had not heard her speak in tongues. She tried hard to speak. Concerned members coaxed her, urged her on and prayed for her. She had to admit that she did not quite have it. Time was running out. Cancer was attacking her body, but her agony was not physical; it was spiritual and mental.

One day in desperation she asked this Methodist preacher, "What can I do? I don't want to go to hell!" I was her boss in a secular position in an institution full of heathens. But, I was a preacher — a jackleg preacher — but a preacher nevertheless. I resisted the temptation to discuss my view of hell. It was not important. The issue was God's grace and God's goodness. God's glorious plan for the salvation of this dear sister was all that mattered. So, I told her to turn to Romans 10:9 and give herself the test. "Is Jesus your Lord? Do you believe that God raised him from the dead?" She answered these questions in the affirmative. I told her, "Be assured my sister, you are saved. If you speak in tongues, you are saved. If you don't speak in tongues, you are saved. If you believe in a burning hell, you are saved. If you don't believe in a burning hell, you are saved." If you confess with your mouth, "Jesus is Lord," and believe in your heart that God raised him from the dead, you will be saved. (Romans 10:9). She died a few months later with the calm assurance that she was saved and prepared to meet her Savior and Lord.

John records an instance when Jesus dealt with his disciples' concerns about someone else's eternal fate. When Peter saw him, he asked, "Lord, what about him?" Jesus answered, "If I want him to remain alive until I return, what is that to you? You must follow me." (John 21:21-22). Peter asked Jesus, "What about him?" Jesus answered (Glenn's paraphrased version), "None of your business. Do what I ask of you." In other words, Jesus said to his disciple that he should not worry about what is going to happen to someone else. Instead, he should focus on his duty to follow Jesus.

A well-known television personality recently did a special program about heaven. She asked one of the ministers interviewed if a person who does not believe in Jesus Christ is going to hell. The minister hesitated for a brief moment and then answered, "Yes."   My first reaction to his response was that I appreciated his honesty and directness. Too many people have danced around this issue in an attempt to be sensitive, inclusive or politically correct. Christians who sincerely hold this belief should say so without equivocation or hesitation. I am sure that the following, among other scriptures, should give them great confidence that their point of view is correct. *"Salvation is found in no one else, for there is no other name under heaven given to men by which we must be saved."* *(Acts 4:12)*. This does not mean that Gandhi is in hell. Gandhi's fate is not our business any more than John's fate was Peter's. It means that God gave us a name that we may invoke for healing and salvation. God is still sovereign and will save whomever God chooses, even those who do not use the precious name of Jesus.

I was listening recently to a preacher on the radio who was talking about the merciful nature of God while insisting that God has to punish people. He argued that if there were no punishment, God wouldn't be a just Father. The preacher described heavenly joys along with eternal punishment and damnation.   "God's justice demands that God must punish us", he argued.   I thought then that God, as the head of this family into which you and I have been adopted by believing in Jesus Christ, is not a just God. I'm thankful that God is not just, because justice would mean that God would give me what I deserve. If God gave me what I deserve, then indeed I can only look forward to punishment and being pushed out of the family. *He does not treat us as our sins deserve or repay us according to our iniquities.* (Psalm 103:10). God is a God of grace who demonstrated such love for the family of God that all we have to do is believe in Jesus to become joint heirs with Jesus.

No true characteristic of God is ever associated with the word "but." We never hear "God is omnipotent, *but* there is one area where God is powerless. God is omniscient, *but* there are some areas where God lacks wisdom. God is omnipresent, *but* there are some places where God cannot be." The only exception to this rule is when some people describe God's love. They have been heard to say "God is love, *but* God is a God of wrath" or "God is love, *but* God is a God of justice." God's occasional expressions of wrath and persistent pursuit of justice cannot stand in opposition to God's lovingly kind character. Nothing stands in opposition to the love of God. God is love. Period! There are no ifs, ands, or buts. God's love is an unconditional part of the character of God.

It seems clear that Jesus did in fact believe in and warn against hell. However, he clearly taught that hell is a place of eternal destruction. *Do not be afraid of those who kill the body but cannot kill the soul. Rather, be afraid of the One who can destroy both soul and body in hell. (Matthew 10:28).* Once this destruction (annihilation) occurs it is eternal. That is, it cannot be undone. The psalmist records this same idea. *Though the wicked spring up like grass and all evildoers flourish, they will be forever destroyed.* (Psalm 92:7). Paul weighs in with his own ominous warnings. *He will punish those who do not know God and do not obey the gospel of our Lord Jesus. They will be punished with everlasting destruction and shut out from the presence of the Lord and from the majesty of his power.* (2 Thessalonians 1:8-9). Peter seems to express the same idea about destruction: *By the same word the present heavens and earth are reserved for fire, being kept for the day of judgment and destruction of ungodly men. (2 Peter 3:7).*

The good news is that heaven is as real as hell. Jesus said, *"And if I go and prepare a place for you, I will come back and take you to be with me that you also may be where I am." (John 14:3).* Believers don't have to worry about someone sending them to hell. Christians have the assurance of salvation. God is sovereign. God can save even me if God chooses to do so, even if I am wrong about hell, if I am wrong about baptism, if I don't speak in tongues, if I am wrong about any ritual of the church, and if I belong to the wrong denomination. I believe that Christ was raised from the dead. He is my Lord. Therefore, he promised me that even I will be saved.

Chapter 8

WHAT KIND OF LOVE IS THIS?

When they had finished eating, Jesus said to Simon Peter,
"Simon son of John, do you truly love me more than these?"
(John 21:15).

I often closed my radio broadcast by saying, "We would love to hear from you." One week a listener finally wrote me a letter. That was an exciting day as my secretary placed the unopened letter on my desk. I noticed that it did not have a return address, but that didn't lessen my enthusiasm as I almost tore the letter open. I scanned the letter quickly and noticed that it did not have a signature. But, I thought, maybe the writer is shy and modest and prefers to remain anonymous. I soon realized that this was not exactly a letter expressing Christian love for me or mine. I must admit, however, that the thing that impressed me most was not the aspersions cast on me or my family heritage. It was the fact that the writer said that I am "BORING." The writer suggested that other radio preachers are exciting, have a sweet whoop and make them feel good. I know what the writer means, because no one appreciates a preacher who has mastered the art of skillful delivery, blessed by resonant tones, more than I. But God did not give me that or call me to preach that way. Instead, God told me to "study to show myself approved and rightly divide the word of truth." If you want a quick, feel good experience, then buy a good ice cream cone in the summer or a cup of hot chocolate in winter. But, if you want an everlasting feel good experience, open your mind to understand and meditate on the goodness and the love of God.   I must warn you that this discussion may be especially difficult for those who look for the quick rise to exciting heights, because we must talk a little bit about Greek. That's right, Greek, the language in which the New Testament was written. But please, hang in through this BORING chapter.

John records a post-resurrection experience where Jesus invited his disciples to share in a meal with him. He then proceeded to ask Peter a simple but very direct question, *"Do you love me?" (John 21:15).* This is not a mysterious or complex question. It could have been answered with a simple "yes" or "no." The English translation, in fact, has Peter giving that kind of answer: He said, "Yes. *I love you."* But you knew that it couldn't be that simple. I said that we have to use our mind and go a little deeper. Back in seminary days, I studied four courses in Greek. I even passed two of them. So that qualifies me, of course, to make the following observation. According to the Greek text, Jesus used a word for love that has the same root as "agape" in agape feast. This is the highest kind of spiritual love. It is the root of the word used in the love verse, *John 3:16,* in the love chapter, *1 Corinthians 13,* and in the love letter, *1 John.* Even in *1 John* when John writes about brotherly love, "agape" is used.

Therefore, it is with great interest that we realize that Peter's answer to Jesus after the first question was *"Yes, Lord I love you,"* but the word in Greek has the root for phileo, brotherly love. In other words, Jesus was asking "Do you love me like God loves?"   Peter answered "Yes, I love you like a brother." Men, this is equivalent to your wife asking you, "Do you love me?" followed by your answer, "Yes, dear. I have great affection for you." Just grab your pillow and head straight for the couch!

Jesus asked Simon a second time, *"Do you love (agape) me?"* Simon answered, *"Yes, Lord I love (phileo) you."* Each time Jesus gave a commandment, *"Feed those little ones who follow me."* Peter was getting a little irritated by this time. Why did the Lord insist on asking the same question when he had been given a clear answer? Jesus persisted, but this time the Greek reveals a surprise. Jesus changed the question. In English it sounds the same: *"Do you love me?"* But in New Testament Greek the question is now *"Do you love (phileo) me?"* Jesus was saying that he tried to get Peter to come up to his high spiritual plane. Peter insisted on an earthly answer. So, Jesus re-phrased the question, "Do you even love me like a brother?" Yet, Jesus was clearly saying that even if that was the best Peter could do, he still could not escape Christ's commandment: *"Feed my sheep!"*

Simon Peter must have been thinking, "What kind of love is this?" The resurrected Jesus was saying, "This love drove me back to Jerusalem when you advised me to stay away. Love let me hold my peace when the torturers abused me. This love let me be nailed to the cross to die for you." What kind of love is this? *"Greater love has no man than this; to lay down his life for his friends."* *(John 15:13)*. Do you love him with agape love? Then he commands you to feed his sheep.

This is not the end of this love business. Men do not easily express love toward other men. Some expressions of love by men toward men make modern-day men very uncomfortable. We don't show love and we certainly don't express it. The fear for most straight men is that someone might think they are gay. The fear for many gay men is that someone might think they are gay. If love is expressed, it must have "man" at the end. That somehow softens the phrase, or at least makes it acceptable. A real man would never say to another man, "I love you." But, he could say, "I love you, man."

David and Jonathan spoke and demonstrated great love for each other. Jonathan did a virtual striptease as he took off his royal outer garments and his sword, his bow, and his belt, and gave them to David to seal the covenant between them. There is no doubt in the minds of many men, that such a profuse expression on the part of Jonathan can only be an indication of homosexual desires. Surely, they think, this kind of "love" is just an intense same-sex lust. It may be blasphemously painful to think of David, the "man after God's own heart" this way. But surely, they believe, only the spiritually naive can draw any other conclusion.

David, however, in his passionate eulogy for Jonathan, clearly indicated that their love was neither sexual nor perverse. David loved women in the most intense sexual and romantic way. His love for Jonathan was fuller, deeper, and of a different character than that. He said after Jonathan's death that their love was *"wonderful, more wonderful than that of women." (2 Samuel 1:26)*. In other words, this love was not the same kind as his sexual love for women. In fact, their love was not sexual at all in the routine, mundane sense. It was more, much more.

Part of the discomfort for those of us who believe in Jesus as our Lord and Savior is the fact that Jesus, like David, was not afraid or ashamed to show love toward other men. The rich young ruler inquired of Jesus, *"What must I do to inherit eternal life?" (Mark 10:17)*. This question came from a man who already had a pretty good temporal life. He had status in society, wealth, and, we presume, women. Was his quest for life beyond his very comfortable earthly life merely the selfish request of one who had a lot and wanted more? Had he been impressed and moved by the magnificent and miraculous works of Jesus? We can't be sure, but we know that something drove him to Jesus to ask the fateful question. Mark records Jesus' reaction to this wealthy man, *"He looked at him and loved him."* *(Mark 10:19).* What kind of love is this? What caused Mark to describe the deep compassion that Jesus felt for this man as "love?" Agape is the word given in the original Greek.

Jesus explained to the man that he was so close to the Kingdom. The only thing that he needed to do was to reciprocate. That is, he needed to show that his love for Jesus was as great as Jesus' love for him. He could do this easily by taking the material things that obscure that love, and giving them to the poor. The man was distressed and distraught. He could not do what the disciples did. He could not leave everything and follow Jesus. He was very sad as he went on his way, alone.

Jesus loved the sibling trio Mary, Martha and Lazarus. He wept openly as he expressed his sorrow on the occasion of Lazarus' death and the obvious distress of his sisters. He was not concerned about what other men would think, or about the community's reaction to his unmanly tears and expressions of grief. He truly became one of us and dwelt among us as a man, with the full human range of emotions. He loved Lazarus deeply and was not ashamed to show it.

It is not difficult to explain away the love that Jesus had for the rich young ruler and for Lazarus. One is closely akin to sincere compassion and the other mimics the love that one has for brothers and sisters. There is no funny business going on here. John, however, presents a different problem. What kind of love is this? First of all, there appears to have been a physical closeness not described in the other relationships. John leaned on Jesus. The mental picture comes perilously close to cuddling and caressing. It's true that each disciple had to invade another's space in order to eat the common meal. However, they seemed to recognize that Jesus' relationship to John was sufficiently different that they called John the disciple whom Jesus "loved." What kind of love is this? After all, Jesus expressed love for all of them and commanded that they love one another as the most important sign that they were his followers.

Some scholars suggest that John may have been much younger than the other disciples, and as such, was regarded as a beloved younger brother by Jesus and the others. They would have been much more protective and nurturing of him than the other rough and hardened tradesmen and businessmen. This brotherly relationship was so close, that it was to John that Jesus entrusted the future welfare of his mother as he felt his life slipping away on the cross. This is especially striking in light of the fact that Jesus had other brothers and sisters in Joseph's extended household.

I had an occasion to reflect on this man-to-man love in a most unexpected way in recent months. I had been ill with various physical ailments that had caused me for the first time in thirty-five years in the pastorate to miss time from the pulpit and the office. I overcame my reticence and natural shyness to share a little of my struggle with the congregation. This became necessary, because some of the conditions generated pain that could not be hidden from my face, and made it difficult for me to move in my normally spry way.

One of the brothers in the congregation called me at home to inquire about my health and to share the fact that he was facing at least some of the same issues. He had guessed that when I mentioned that the doctors had ordered a biopsy that I might be dealing with the same test for cancer that he would soon endure. He was correct. Since this was his first test, I described in my crude and rude way what he could expect, while ensuring him that the discomfort was great, but the pain was bearable and that he would survive.

He wanted me to know that he was praying for me and that God had placed on his heart the assurance that I would come through this ordeal unscathed and have more opportunities to be a faithful witness and servant of God. I received a great deal of comfort from his words. However, he said something as he hung up the phone that was very unsettling and unnerving. He was supposed to say "I'll be praying for you" or "You will be in my prayers." My response, "God bless you." had left my mouth before I realized that he had softly said, "I love you." Those words rang in my ears as I instinctively followed through on the motion of hanging up the phone. I wondered if he realized what he had said, or if he had inadvertently ended our conversation with the words reserved for his wife or children. I will never know, because I don't have the nerve to ask him.

I needed to hear, as I awaited the results of the biopsy, that I am loved. This godly man spoke the words that real men only reluctantly speak, even to their wives or lovers. He spoke them to a man, a brother in Christ who needed to hear them at that moment. He even avoided the formula and did not dilute the impact by adding "man" at the end. He did not say the acceptable, "I love you, man." He said the powerful and risky, "I love you." This is an example of how the Holy Spirit enables godly men and women to express the love of God in fully understandable ways.

MEN

God's concern for men is deep. The next two chapters deal in a special way with men. This is not surprising since most of the Bible focuses on the actions of godly and godless men. The first of these two chapters uses the story of Zacchaeus to show how a man can move from a place of legalistic hypocrisy to an understanding of a Messiah who could bring salvation to his house.

The second chapter shows that Jesus was zealous in his concern for the special men who were his disciples. He reminded them on occasion that they did not choose him; he chose them and he was determined that he would keep them in his fold.

Chapter 9

THE MAN IN A TREE

Jesus entered Jericho and was passing through. A man was there by the name of Zacchaeus; he was a chief tax collector and was wealthy. He wanted to see who Jesus was, but being a short man he could not, because of the crowd. So he ran ahead and climbed a sycamore-fig tree to see him, since Jesus was coming that way. When Jesus reached the spot, he looked up and said to him, "Zacchaeus, come down immediately. I must stay at your house today." So he came down at once and welcomed him gladly. All the people saw this and began to mutter, "He has gone to be the guest of a 'sinner.' " But Zacchaeus stood up and said to the Lord, "Look, Lord! Here and now I give half of my possessions to the poor, and if I have cheated anybody out of anything, I will pay back four times the amount." Jesus said to him, "Today salvation has come to this house, because this man, too, is a son of Abraham. For the Son of Man came to seek and to save what was lost." (Luke 19:1-10).

Zacchaeus was a wealthy man. That was not a bad thing in and of itself. The problem was not his wealth. It was the way that he got his wealth. A tax collector collected money for the Roman government--a government that forced its citizens to worship the emperor as an idol god. The tax collector made his money by extorting all that he could after he had collected the taxes due the government. Zacchaeus was very good at his business. He was the chief tax collector. Despite all that Zacchaeus had done wrong, he apparently was trying to do at least one thing right; he wanted to see who Jesus was. He must have heard people talking about this new prophet, rabbi, preacher and teacher. He must have heard that Jesus was passing through Jericho.

The Bible doesn't tell us how Zacchaeus heard about Jesus. But, other scriptures tell us that there were people who spread the word about the miracles performed by Jesus. *Now the crowd that was with him when he called Lazarus from the tomb and raised him from the dead continued to spread the word. Many people, because they had heard that he had given this miraculous sign, went out to meet him. So the Pharisees said to one another, "See, this is getting us nowhere. Look how the whole world has gone after him!" Now there were some Greeks among those who went up to worship at the Feast. They came to Philip, who was from Bethsaida in Galilee, with a request. "Sir," they said, "we would like to see Jesus." (John 12:17-21).*

Many of us share Zacchaeus' problem. The Bible tells us that he was a short man who couldn't see Jesus because of the crowd. We want to see Jesus, too, but we can't see him because of the crowd of folk blocking the view. Many of these people were true disciples of Jesus. They just wanted to be around him to hear every word that he spoke and watch how he did things. They may have been in the crowd because they wanted something from Jesus for themselves. Some might have been in the crowd because they were among the spies who were sent by the opposition to record and report every one of Jesus' actions. But I'll bet you that not many of his true disciples realized that their presence in the crowd might prevent someone else from seeing Jesus. Some people, like Zacchaeus, have to climb up high onto a different plane and look over the crowd before they are able to see Jesus. One can't see Jesus, unless one can look beyond the crowd that has him boxed in.

Many people who claim to be followers of Jesus,

who are in the crowd that surrounds Jesus, don't want
Jesus to have anything to do with anyone else. Many
sincere Christians are like that. They say that no one can
get near Jesus unless he or she becomes part of their
crowd. Zacchaeus had to run ahead of the crowd and
climb a tree. Jesus looked up and said, *"Come down
immediately. I must stay at your house today." (Luke 19:5).*
Jesus spoke loudly so that the whole crowd heard him.
Zacchaeus was happy as he came down and greeted
Jesus. But the crowd began to murmur about Jesus. *"He
has gone to be the guest of a sinner." (Luke 19:7)).*

Zacchaeus was now on the defensive. Jesus was
being attacked for his recognition of him, so he
responded by making an offer to Jesus. *"Look, Lord! Here
and now I give half of my possessions to the poor, and if I have
cheated anybody out of anything, I will pay back four times the
amount." (Luke 19:8).* Giving half of his ill-gotten wealth
to the poor meant that he would still be a very wealthy
man. Maybe he also thought of the Hebrew scripture,
*Blessed is he who considers the poor; The LORD will deliver
him in time of trouble. (Psalm 41:1, NKJV).* The law
required that *when he thus sins and becomes guilty, he must
return what he has stolen or taken by extortion, or what was
entrusted to him, or the lost property he found, or whatever it
was he swore falsely about. He must make restitution in full,
add a fifth of the value to it and give it all to the owner on the
day he presents his guilt offering. (Leviticus 6:4-5).* In other
words, when he came to God to present his guilt offering
for lying, he was required to pay the man back and add a
penalty of one fifth. This requirement is affirmed with an
additional requirement that the offender *must confess the
sin he has committed. He must make full restitution for his
wrong, add one fifth to it and give it all to the person he has
wronged. (Numbers 5:7).*

Some commentators suggest that the expression
"if I have cheated," should be read, "since I have cheated".

One did not get to be chief tax collector without lying, cheating, and coercing. This confession may have been the most difficult part of Zacchaeus' offer. Many of us have made this kind of half-hearted confession that surely is not pleasing to God. "Well, if I said anything to offend you, I am sorry. If I hurt your feelings, I'm sorry. But you shouldn't be so sensitive." An expression that starts with the conditional phrase "If I..." is not confession. True confession begins with the direct, affirmative, sorrowful statement, "I have sinned." "I have stolen." "I have lied." "I am sorry." The law also said that a thief (Zacchaeus certainly was a thief) of sheep had to *"restore fourfold."* *"If a man steals an ox or a sheep and slaughters it or sells it, he must pay back five head of cattle for the ox and four sheep for the sheep."* (Exodus 22:1).

Zacchaeus did a lot of talking at this dinner. Then it was Jesus' turn. First he said, *"Today salvation has come to this house..."* (Luke 19:9). Jesus is the Savior, but he did not say, "Today the Savior has come to this house." Jesus' presence in the house, while life-changing, did not bring salvation. Salvation comes to those who believe in the present Savior and demonstrate that belief by their confession of faith and actions. Zacchaeus said in effect, "Jesus, because of you, I am going to act like a true son of Abraham." Zacchaeus had not lived up to the requirements of the law until he had his encounter with Jesus.

It was not Zacchaeus' genetic lineage or his birthright that made him a son of Abraham. It was his new-found willingness to live up to the Abrahamic principles of justice and fair play that made it possible for Jesus to declare that Zacchaeus was a son of Abraham and -- most important of all -- saved. The *Gospel According to Luke* summarizes that *"For the Son of Man came to seek and to save what was lost."* (Luke 19:10). How

was Zacchaeus lost?   He came from a good family.   He
was a son of Abraham.   How did he get lost?   He craved
money and, as the chief tax collector, he worshiped the
emperor.

Jesus had preached against this kind of worship
throughout his ministry.   *"Do not store up for yourselves*
treasures on earth, where moth and rust destroy, and where
thieves break in and steal.   But store up for yourselves
treasures in heaven, where moth and rust do not destroy, and
where thieves do not break in and steal.   For where your
treasure is, there your heart will be also."   (Matthew 6 :19-21).
Zacchaeus looked from his tree-high perch, saw the Son
of God, believed and found salvation.   Many of us are up
in a tree looking down, over and beyond the crowd,
trying to get a glimpse of Jesus.   He beckons to you to
come down out of your tree, come unto him, believe and
live.

Chapter 10

LET THESE MEN GO!

So Judas came to the grove, guiding a detachment of soldiers and some officials from the chief priests and Pharisees. They were carrying torches, lanterns and weapons. Jesus, knowing all that was going to happen to him, went out and asked them, "Who is it you want?" "Jesus of Nazareth," they replied. "I am he," Jesus said. (And Judas the traitor was standing there with them.) When Jesus said, "I am he," they drew back and fell to the ground. Again he asked them, "Who is it you want?" And they said, "Jesus of Nazareth." "I told you that I am he," Jesus answered. "If you are looking for me, then let these men go." (John 18:3-8).

Jesus and his disciples sat around the table eating when he changed the meaning of the ceremonial meal that they had eaten in times past. He said, *"This is my body..."* and *"This is my blood..."* Think anew about what Jesus might have meant when he said, *"This is my body."* Paul often tried to explain this idea to the church. *Just as each of us has one body with many members, and these members do not all have the same function, so in Christ we who are many form one body, and each member belongs to all the others. (Romans 12:4,5).* In fact, Jesus' most persistent prayer for his disciples was that they might be united in love for each other and him. Paul understood the pivotal importance of this idea as he repeated it throughout his writings. *So that there should be no division in the body, but that its parts should have equal concern for each other. If one part suffers, every part suffers with it; if one part is honored, every part rejoices with it. Now you are the body of Christ, and each one of you is a part of it. (1 Cor. 12:25-27).*

Jesus was not his usual jovial and social self on that night. He seemed so introspective, downright moody on this particular occasion. They sang a hymn, went out and eventually made their way to the Mount of Olives where they would often go to retreat and pray. Recently, my bishop called the pastors together for a retreat. We were reminded by the speakers that the devil knows where you go to get away and is still lurking around trying to prevent you from getting the rest that will allow you to be rejuvenated. John records the actions of Judas Iscariot after the devil entered him. *Now Judas, who betrayed him, knew the place, because Jesus had often met there with his disciples. So Judas came to the grove, guiding a detachment of soldiers and some officials from the chief priests and Pharisees. (John 18:2,3).* A group of people showed up with torches and lanterns and even weapons. They obviously had not come for the prayer service. They had not come to this worship group to join in the praise of God. Some people show up at the place of worship armed with the tools of destruction. They are not always outsiders. Sometimes they are led by an insider like Judas, the one who handled the money and had his own vision of where this movement should go, a place different from where Jesus, the Messianic leader had determined.

Jesus then stepped out of the garden and asked the critical question, *"Who is it you want?"* Jesus moved to the front just as he had done when he rushed to the head of this band as it paraded on the way to Jerusalem for the last time. He led the way as he demonstrated what our ancestors often proclaimed, "He is God all by himself!" *"I am he," Jesus said. (And Judas the traitor was standing there with them.) When Jesus said, "I am he," they drew back and fell to the ground. (John 18:5,6).* It's not obvious to me why they drew back and fell to the ground. We know that the Bible promises *that at the name of Jesus every knee should bow, in heaven and on earth and under the earth, and every tongue confess that Jesus Christ is Lord. (Philippians 2:10-11).* Even these unwitting agents of the devil found themselves falling to their knees at the mention of Jesus' name.

Again he asked them, "Who is it you want?" And they said, "Jesus of Nazareth." "I told you that I am he," Jesus answered. "If you are looking for me, then let these men go." (John 18:7-8). Luke tells us that Jesus had warned the disciples that this day would come. *"Simon, Simon, Satan has asked to sift you as wheat. But I have prayed for you, Simon, that your faith may not fail. And when you have turned back, strengthen your brothers." (Luke 22:31-32).* Jesus' concern for his disciples was on clear display. These are the ones who would have to build his church. The devil could not have them. The devil was not satisfied to get Jesus. He wanted to destroy the church. They have imperfect faith, incomplete faith, weak faith but he had declared that upon this faith in him he would build his church. *Let these men go!*

Jesus had often expressed his prayerful concern about protecting his disciples and his determination that the devil would not take them away from him either while he was with them or after he ascended. *And this is the will of him who sent me, that I shall lose none of all that he has given me, but raise them up at the last day. (John 6:39). I give them eternal life, and they shall never perish; no one can snatch them out of my hand. (John 10:28). While I was with them, I protected them and kept them safe by that name you gave me. None has been lost except the one doomed to destruction so that Scripture would be fulfilled. (John 17:12). This happened so that the words he had spoken would be fulfilled: "I have not lost one of those you gave me." (John 18:9).*

Jesus was saying that they could take his physical body. They could bruise him and wound him. But they could not have the body of Christ, THE CHURCH. *Now you are the body of Christ, and each one of you is a part of it. (1 Cor. 12:27).* God had written in the scrolls, *"Do not touch my anointed ones; do my prophets no harm." (Psalm 105:15).* Furthermore, he knew that *God is our refuge and strength, an ever-present help in trouble. Therefore we will not fear, though the earth give way and the mountains fall into the heart of the sea, though its waters roar and foam and the mountains quake with their surging. (Psalm 46:1-3).*

Jesus is asking those who would destroy his body, those who would sift us and divide us, "Do you think that you are going to take my body and destroy my church? Do you think that you are going to snatch these that I have called and anointed out of my hand? You cannot have my body. Let these men go." Those who would destroy the church should reflect on the psalmist's declaration, *"Be still, and know that I am God; I will be exalted among the nations, I will be exalted in the earth." The* LORD *Almighty is with us; the God of Jacob is our fortress. (Psalm 46:10-11).*

WOMEN

The Bible was written and compiled by many inspired men and (perhaps a few) women. The role of man is so central that God is usually viewed as male and the key players are male with the other gender having a subordinate role. The next three chapters are designed to provoke dialogue about the gender question. They don't attempt a scholarly examination of gender roles. Instead, they look to the word of God as source material for deeper reflections about this matter.

Chapter 11

AND

After this, Jesus traveled about from one town and village to another, proclaiming the good news of the kingdom of God. The Twelve were with him, and also some women who had been cured of evil spirits and diseases: Mary (called Magdalene) from whom seven demons had come out; Joanna the wife of Cuza, the manager of Herod's household; Susanna; and many others. These women were helping to support them out of their own means. (Luke 8:1-3).

My Greek professor was an excellent and enthusiastic teacher who delighted in pointing out the intricacies of the language. He took special pleasure in describing one three-letter word that has particular significance, "Kai," spelled kappa alpha iota. He pronounced it the same as the "ki" in the word "kite." It means that the phrase that comes before it is not the end of the thought. There is more to follow. Kai is a conjunction that is most often translated into English as "and." Its purpose is to connect two or more phrases that have equal weight or value.

Jesus often traveled *about from one town and village to another, proclaiming the good news of the kingdom of God. (Luke 8:1).* Some of us forget that Jesus was first and foremost a preacher who proclaimed and demonstrated the good news by healing the sick and driving out demons. *The Book of Luke* points out in a very matter-of-fact way that Jesus was not alone. The Twelve were there. That was no surprise. *Mark* records their names and their mission to heal the sick and cast out demons. *Jesus went up on a mountainside and called to him those he wanted, and they came to him. He appointed twelve--designating them apostles--that they might be with him and that he might send them out to preach and to have authority to drive out demons. (Mark 3:13-15).* There were many disciples who followed Jesus, but only twelve who he sent out as apostles.

For many people this is the end of the story. They have seen all of the pictures. Great artists throughout the ages painted the pictures of the last supper. Jesus and the twelve disciples are shown clearly; usually no one else is there. Many movies of the last few decades present the same scenario.

The Book of Luke follows the mention of the Twelve with the three-letter conjunction, *"and,"* as he wrote in this passage: *"and also some women who had been cured of evil spirits and diseases: Mary (called Magdalene) from whom seven demons had come out." (Luke 8:2).* The women did not suddenly appear or materialize. They were there all along, next to and in support of the men and their holy mission. Their role was different from the male disciples, but of equal value, as shown by the connecting conjunction, "kai" in the original Greek.

These women who supported Jesus and his male disciples were very special because they were freed from their evil spirits. There is no mention of the demons in the men. We can't be sure whether the men were or were not still demon-possessed. We do know, however, that the demons that possessed the women had been exorcised. It was important for this to be mentioned since believers needed to know that no evil women need apply. These women were spiritually clean and had no corrupting influences on Jesus or his disciples.

The first woman mentioned was *Mary (called Magdalene) from whom seven demons had come out.* Mary Magdalene is the center of many modern-day religious controversies. She has been called everything from Jesus' disciple to lover and wife. Some traditions of the early church said that she was a prostitute, though there is no such indication in the scriptures. She was demonized by some in the church, which is ironic since her demons were exorcised. It is clear, however, that she was a close and valued member of the Jesus movement.

Joanna the wife of Cuza, the manager of Herod's household, was mentioned next. She was another man's wife and (we presume) a mother who had her own family that needed care. Yet, she supported Jesus financially in Galilee and was named as a witness to the empty tomb after the resurrection. Many husbands understand the strain that can accompany enabling a dedicated wife to serve the needs of the church, while longing for her to pay more attention to home. Her husband was the administrator of Herod Antipas' domestic affairs. He would have been in a position to talk to the king about the great rabbi and prophet who was preaching and healing in Galilee. Cuza might have been the one who gave Herod the news about Jesus: *Now Herod the tetrarch heard about all that was going on. And he was perplexed, because some were saying that John had been raised from the dead, others that Elijah had appeared, and still others that one of the prophets of long ago had come back to life. But Herod said, "I beheaded John. Who, then, is this I hear such things about?" And he tried to see him. (Luke 9:7-9).*

Susanna was Hebrew. Her name is the same as Lily in Greek. We don't know much about her, except that she was present at the beginning and helped to support Jesus financially. She is not listed by name at the resurrection.

The Bible is clear. There were many other women who were disciples of Jesus. Only twelve special men were called apostles, but many men and women were called disciples. The Twelve were businessmen or government officials with prominent places in Galilean society. Most had wives and families who often traveled with them. Paul pointed out that women were an integral part of the post-resurrection church. *Don't we have the right to take a believing wife along with us, as do the other apostles and the Lord's brothers and Cephas? (1 Corinthians 9:5).* The women were there at the beginning, along the journey, and after the resurrection.

Mary Magdalene was the first to give the triumphant cry *"I have seen the Lord!" (John 20:18).* The women were there in the presence of Jesus and the apostles. They were not just in the back room preparing to serve meals and playing a secondary role. Jesus spoke with them directly. We know this because an angel reminded them of what they heard Jesus say. *Remember how he told you, while he was still with you in Galilee. The Son of Man must be delivered into the hands of sinful men, be crucified and on the third day be raised again. Then they remembered his words. (Luke 24:6-8).*

Many women were there watching from a distance. These women remained faithful and active, though they normally were relegated to obscure positions. They remained determined, though they were air-brushed out of the picture. They remained supportive, even when their names were not called and they served in anonymity. *Many other women who had come up with him to Jerusalem were also there. (Mark 15:41).*

In our churches we celebrate Men's Day and Women's Day, Mother's Day and Father's Day. I have no criticism of special opportunities to recognize the particular contributions of persons of each gender. We must never forget, however, that the Bible declares that *in the Lord, however, woman is not independent of man, nor is man independent of woman. For as woman came from man, so also man is born of woman. But everything comes from God. (1 Corinthians 11:11-12).* Paul summed up the matter directly and succinctly when the Holy Spirit caused him to write, *There is neither Jew nor Greek, slave nor free, male nor female, for you are all one in Christ Jesus.* *(Galatians 3:28).*

The disciples had a difficult time believing what Jesus had promised them. Might it have been because the good news was announced by the women who they viewed as being there in a subordinate role? Jesus had demonstrated many times how much he valued the women who supported his mission. It is apparent that the male disciples had not acquired the same level of respect and trust to believe these women were bearers of the truth. *When they came back from the tomb, they told all these things to the Eleven and to all the others. It was Mary Magdalene, Joanna, Mary the mother of James, and the others with them who told this to the apostles. But they did not believe the women, because their words seemed to them like nonsense.* *(Luke 24:9-11).*

One of my sisters in the pastoral ministry told me recently that she must send one of her male ministerial associates to certain functions in her community, because the male pastors in the community will not fellowship with her or accept her prophetic witness. Moreover, some of the men in a nearby community have threatened to send a delegation of men to her church to "straighten out" her congregation for allowing a woman to exert authority over the men.

When we challenge women who are called to service, we are really challenging God's sovereignty. Who are we to tell God who God can call to meet the needs of God's people? Who are we to tell women that they must remain at a distance, or be silent with their heads covered and their eyes downcast? Thank God that when men said "no," God said "yes." When people said "exclude," God said "include." When people said "except", God said "accept"; most of all, when people said "but," God said "and." And the poor, and the disabled, and the Samaritan, and the Jew, and the Gentile, and you, and me, and the women, and...

Chapter 12

LESSONS FROM TWO OUTCAST WOMEN

While he was in Bethany, reclining at the table in the home of a man known as Simon the Leper, a woman came with an alabaster jar of very expensive perfume, made of pure nard. She broke the jar and poured the perfume on his head. Some of those present were saying indignantly to one another, "Why this waste of perfume? It could have been sold for more than a year's wages and the money given to the poor." And they rebuked her harshly. "Leave her alone," said Jesus. "Why are you bothering her? She has done a beautiful thing to me. The poor you will always have with you, and you can help them any time you want. But you will not always have me. She did what she could. She poured perfume on my body beforehand to prepare for my burial. (Mark 14:3-8).

Just then a woman who had been subject to bleeding for twelve years came up behind him and touched the edge of his cloak. She said to herself, "If I only touch his cloak, I will be healed." Jesus turned and saw her. "Take heart, daughter," he said, "your faith has healed you." And the woman was healed from that moment. (Matthew 9:20-22).

This story about the woman who was in Bethany at the house of Simon the leper is a very well known story about a woman who we think we know. I've heard some very powerful sermons preached on this scripture, especially by our sister clergy. Jesus and his disciples sat around a table eating, and engaged in the usual dinnertime small talk. Jesus was explaining to the men his purposes for coming into the world. Dinner guests didn't sit in chairs the way we would today. They didn't have regular plates and silverware. In order to eat at this table, one had to lean, recline, and invade a neighbor's space. The custom was to lean on the left arm leaving the right hand free to reach over and grab a piece of bread or meat. Depending on where a disciple sat, he might even be able to lean on Jesus. They could not do what they had to do in isolation nor could they be sensitive to someone else's touch.

A woman came in. We can be pretty sure that this woman was not welcome at the table. Neither, most likely, was any other woman. This was a very rude thing for her to do. It violated etiquette and social protocol. She had a special container of oil. The scripture doesn't tell us how she got the oil. We don't know if she got the oil by doing something that she should not have done. It is apparent that it was very valuable to her.

The disciples were shocked and a little irritated with this woman. I'm sure they were thinking that she was supposed to be back in the kitchen preparing to serve them. This woman had some nerve to come in and disturb the men's conversation with Jesus just as they were solving all the great problems of the world. Her reputation may have been a little suspect in the first place. She removed any doubt when she poured the flask of oil onto Jesus' head in such a wasteful way. Nevertheless, we can learn a lot from her.

Jesus said two things about the woman's action that lead to valuable insight about how to get close to God. The first thing Jesus said in defense of this woman was, *"Leave her alone...She has done a beautiful thing to me."* *(Mark 14:6).* It was obvious that the disciples didn't accept that response from Jesus. They still required further explanation; so Jesus made another comment. He agreed with them that they could have sold the oil and given the money to the poor while reminding them that they would have many opportunities to minister to the poor. Then Jesus said, *"She has done what she could."* *(Mark 14:8).*   What a simple and powerful statement. We don't all have the same resources; we don't always have access to the corridors of power. We often can't pick up the phone and call the people who are the movers and the shakers.   There are times when it's pointless to call the bank because there's nothing in that account.

Jesus was urging his disciples to look and learn a lesson from this woman who was an outsider who could not have a place around the table. She didn't make excuses about what she did not have.   She didn't complain about what she could not do. She did not talk about how she was treated by society. Instead, she did what was in her power to do; she did what she could. A more important lesson from this woman was that when you cannot do anything else, you can praise the Lord. She showed those men who were arguing about who was going to be on the right hand, and who was going to be on the left hand and which one of them was going to be the greatest, how to worship Jesus.

The second narrative about an outcast woman comes from the *9th Chapter of Matthew.* It contains one of the most revealing lessons that one should learn about establishing a relationship with God. I remember as a young boy growing up in Tallahassee, Florida, hearing preachers talk about the woman with the issue of blood. She was automatically an outcast. She was ritually impure according to the law of that time. She couldn't even go to the women's section of the temple to worship. She had taken all her money and gone to the medical quacks trying to find a way to get healed. She heard that if people got close enough to Jesus, he could speak the word of healing and they would be healed. Perhaps in her desperation she felt that she didn't need to get the attention of Jesus but just get close to him so that a miracle could happen for her. She had heard what everybody knew; buying and sacrificing the right animal would get one close to God and possibly get her the healing that she needed. Going to the priest and following the prescribed rituals would also do it. There was no way by law that she could do this.

This woman took the matter of faith in God to a new level. She believed that if she could get close enough to touch the hem of his robe, she could be healed. This woman who was outcast was able to show the society, all the men who were in leadership positions and all of their wives, that if one can get close enough to just touch the hem of his garment, then healing is possible. You can hear her now; you can see her as she fought her way through the crowd. You know she was somewhere in the back. She didn't want to be seen. She didn't want anybody crying out, pointing at her and saying, "unclean," like they did with the lepers. All she wanted to do was be able to just touch the garment. He didn't even have to recognize who she was. Her faith was that strong.

Do you understand that it wasn't her money? It wasn't a ritual that she carried out. It wasn't the priest or the preacher pronouncing the right words. Jesus said, "Your faith has healed you." (Matthew 9:22) She was not clean! She was not holy! She was not righteous! She was not fasting with ashes on her face and sackcloth on her body. She had not gone through any special religious ritual. She had simply acted on her faith, risked the wrath of the crowd and thrust her body forward to touch his garment.

There's one other scripture that I want to call to your attention that often escapes our notice. *And when the men of that place recognized Jesus, they sent word to all the surrounding country. People brought all their sick to him and begged him to let the sick just touch the edge of his cloak, and all who touched him were healed. (Matthew 14:35-36).* Do you understand what has happened? The men who had authority, the men who were leaders of society were coming to Jesus realizing that if they could just touch the hem of his garment like this outcast woman, they could be made whole. No rituals must be performed; no doves have to die; no lambs have to be slaughtered. Just break open the box of precious possessions, worship Jesus with faith and you will be made whole.

Chapter 13

MOTHER MARY'S SUPPORT GROUP

Near the cross of Jesus stood his mother, his mother's sister, Mary the wife of Clopas, and Mary Magdalene. When Jesus saw his mother there, and the disciple whom he loved standing nearby, he said to his mother, "Dear woman, here is your son," and to the disciple, "Here is your mother." From that time on, this disciple took her into his home. (John 19:25-27).

Jesus had begun his journey in Bethlehem and traveled to Nazareth, but it was not complete. He had traveled from Nazareth through Bethany to Jerusalem for the last time; yet, his mission was not finished. He had made a triumphant entry into the city; but his work was not done. He had been convicted in an illegal kangaroo court; yet his journey was not at its end. They nailed him to a cross; yet it was not complete until he saw to it that there was someone to care for his mother. *When Jesus saw his mother there, and the disciple whom he loved standing nearby, he said to his mother, "Dear woman, here is your son," and to the disciple, "Here is your mother."(John 19:26-27).* His mother's future secured, Jesus uttered the prophetic words that had been foretold by the scriptures: *Later, knowing that all was now completed, and so that the Scripture would be fulfilled, Jesus said, "I am thirsty." (John 19:28).*

Any son who has ever been in trouble knows that mother will always be there for him. Mother will not abandon him; she is going to be right in the middle of the action near her beloved son. Not only will she be there, she will bring her support group - her mother, her sisters, her best friend and anyone else who shares in her love for her son. Jesus' mother was there. His aunt was present and possibly his mother's sister-in-law and Mary Magdalene, all of whom were the most precious and dedicated of the many women disciples.

Crucifixion was designed to inflict the most horrific pain. However, the physical pain, no matter how intense, could not match the psychological torment brought by the publicly humiliating spectacle and the victim's knowledge that those most close to him had to stand near for hours, and sometimes days, watching him slowly die. Mother Mary's presence may have been of great comfort to Jesus, yet it was also part of the cruel punishment devised by the Romans. The thought that Mother must endure the embarrassment and pain, only added to the humiliation and anguish. The bodies of those cursed to die by crucifixion were usually thrown on a smoldering garbage dump in Gehenna, where the fires burned day and night and the maggots were plentiful. A family member or friend needed to remain nearby to bribe the soldiers to give them the body so that it could be given a proper burial.

John makes it clear that Mother Mary was not standing alone. The other women were with her near the cross as they had been with her throughout her son's journey from Nazareth. *Near the cross of Jesus stood his mother, his mother's sister, Mary the wife of Clopas, and Mary Magdalene. (John 19:25).* Some of those standing near the cross were very close to Jesus as one can see. Some early historians speculated that Clopas may have been Joseph's brother. This would mean that Mary, the wife of Clopas would have been Mary's sister-in-law, part of the extended family of Jesus. Independent of the familial connection, she was as close as a sister to Mother Mary and was always nearby for support.

There has been much controversy in recent days about Mary Magdalene and Jesus. Some say she was really an apostle or his lover or his wife or the mother of his children. These fanciful speculations are probably good amusement for people with nothing better to do. The Bible is clear, however, that Mary Magdalene was a devoted disciple of Jesus. If she was a fallen woman as some of the men implied, she also was a lifted woman who showed that a person who falls can get up again. If she was an apostle, she demonstrated that she had learned the lessons of humility that Jesus tried to teach the other apostles. She was a servant who came to minister to her beloved Jesus, even as he was dying and after his entombment.

The most important aspect of Mary Magdalene's character, however, is seldom emphasized. She was present with and in support of Mother Mary. She was among those women who humbly and staunchly surrounded Mother Mary as she endured the trauma of watching her beloved son as he was tortured and killed.

The other male disciples, if present, are not mentioned by any of the Gospel writers, unless one considers the implication that Peter may have been lurking around in the shadows. Only John is specifically mentioned by name. Why did this disciple take Mother Mary home? Jesus did not merely tell John to check on his mother every now and then. He did not tell him to provide for her needs from afar. Instead, Jesus said *"Here is your mother"*, which created a much greater obligation for John. Mother Mary would not have been homeless. Even if her husband Joseph was dead, didn't she have other children? Consider the scriptures: *Coming to his hometown, he began teaching the people in their synagogue, and they were amazed. "Where did this man get this wisdom and these miraculous powers?" they asked. "Isn't this the carpenter's son? Isn't his mother's name Mary, and aren't his brothers James, Joseph, Simon and Judas? Aren't all his sisters with us? Where then did this man get all these things?" (Matthew 13:54-56).* Mary apparently had four other sons or stepsons. Some theorize that Joseph was much older than Mary and these brothers were not Mary's sons, but the sons of her older, then deceased husband. They might have had great affection for Mary, but she may not have been their biological mother. This could explain Jesus' desire to be sure that Mary had a son who treated her as an honored mother. John, the beloved disciple fulfilled that role.

Women were indeed powerless in those days and without rights in that society. They needed a connection with a strong man to protect them from abuse and ill treatment. However, there is another possibility to explain Jesus' intentions in establishing this adoptive mother-son relationship between John, who Jesus loved in a special way, and his mother. Mother Mary and the other women had demonstrated that despite the limitations imposed on them by a harsh sexist society, they were able to provide for the needs of Jesus and his disciples out of their own resources. Individually, mothers may have been in peril in that society, but together they were a strong and formidable force. When Jesus said *"Here is your mother,"* he may have been saying that this is the leader of your support group. John would have to help forge the way forward for the forming Christian church. She and her spiritual sisters had followed Jesus from Galilee and supported him and his disciples, and now she would do the same thing for the young disciple, John. All of these women joined with

Jesus' birth mother to remain nearby to meet the needs of Jesus and his disciples.

Many young criminals today look at our mothers and think that they are weak and easy prey for their evil intentions. But they need to take another look. She is not alone. All of her spiritual sisters are standing with her. Not only that, together they are standing near the cross of Jesus. Young mothers need to know that they are no more alone than Mother Mary was alone. They have backup. They have support.

Wars don't end when the last shot is fired. They end when the mothers say "Enough is enough." Real changes don't happen in society because of protest marches. They happen when the mothers decide that they are tired of the status quo. Our society has become increasingly violent in recent years. We decry the lack of respect for others and basic home training of many children. Some young males obviously have been so psychologically castrated that they only feel like men when they carry and use a small firearm as a weapon in a most cowardly way. We shake our heads in anxious disbelief and wonder quietly how their mothers could have failed so miserably. We don't expect much from dad, who often isn't there. But mother is always near her son providing some level of support. The problem is that she so often thinks that she must stand alone. She needs the mothers of the community to show her how to be a mother so that she can provide proper nurture for her wayward son. They shouldn't say, "He's not my son. He's someone else's problem." Her son is our problem.

Jesus from time to time anointed someone to continue his work. Each of the synoptic gospels testifies that he called his disciples to take up their cross and follow him. You can't claim to be a follower of Jesus and fail to carry your cross. Matthew expresses it well. *Then*

Jesus said to his disciples, "If anyone would come after me, he must deny himself and take up his cross and follow me." (Matthew 16:24).

The good news is that you have a support group. Your mother, your aunt, your sisters and their friends are all standing nearby while you bear your cross. They form your spiritual support group. How can they do this? Where do they get their strength and determination? They have taken their stand near the cross of Jesus and their eyes are fixed on him, *the author and perfecter of our faith, who for the joy set before him endured the cross, scorning its shame, and sat down at the right hand of the throne of God. (Hebrews 12:2).*

One of the most famous cries of Jesus from the cross is given in *Psalm 22:1, My God, my God, why have you forsaken me?* Some theologians argue that Jesus never received an answer to his question. They say that he became sin for us, and as such, God had to forsake him. They may be right. However, surely they know that the end of the psalm is not the cry of the forsaken, but a praise hymn from the victorious one who saw the deliverance of the Lord. *Posterity will serve him; future generations will be told about the Lord. They will proclaim his righteousness to a people yet unborn--for he has done it (Psalm 22:30-31).* Jesus knew that he was not alone. He was not forsaken because he looked at the foot of the cross and saw Mother Mary and her support group. God was with him as God is with us when we are obedient, even unto death.

RACE

A former president of the United States recently said that the worst day of his presidency came when an entertainer called him a racist. The entertainer, while not directly using the word "racist", did say that the president did not "care about Black people." Though the claim was probably unfair and unfounded, the president's reaction was most telling about the possibility of honest dialogue about race and class. Thousands of people died during this presidency from terrorist attacks and acts of war. Surely those days of death and suffering were worse than rash name-calling.

This same sensitivity about race prevents those who claim to be religious from acknowledging that "God is no respecter of persons" and that people of every race are included in the heavenly vision. Since I am African American, many of the ideas expressed in the next five chapters reflect my ethnicity and experiences. However, I believe that their application is universal and inclusive.

Chapter 14

REFLECTIONS ON THE SLAVE WOMAN'S SON

Then God said, "Let us make man in our image, in our likeness, and let them rule over the fish of the sea and the birds of the air, over the livestock, over all the earth, and over all the creatures that move along the ground." So God created man in his own image, in the image of God he created him; male and female he created them. God blessed them and said to them, "Be fruitful and increase in number; fill the earth and subdue it. Rule over the fish of the sea and the birds of the air and over every living creature that moves on the ground." (Genesis 1:26-28).

Many people who challenge the inspiration of the Bible point very quickly to the problem of Cain who was afraid that after killing his brother, anyone who saw him would kill him. God put a mark of protection on Cain and declared that anyone who harmed Cain would have to deal with God. Where did these other people come from? Who were the parents of Cain's wife? Traditional conservative biblical exegetes say that Cain's wife must have been his sister. They argue that incest was both necessary and permitted by God in the early stages of human existence during the first generations after creation.

Our theological consciousness has been very influenced by the idea that the harmonized creation stories are in fact one story. Furthermore, this approach seems to discount the notion that those who were told to be *"fruitful and increase in number [multiply, KJV]"* before the description of the creation of Adam and Eve, were part of God's process of creating human beings. *(Genesis 1:28).* Some say that *Chapter 2 of Genesis* merely gives the details of God's sixth day creative activity. Others argue that the *Chapter 1* creatures were not fully human. It is ironic that those who argue for the unified, one creation story idea, are often the same ones who passionately believe in a literal interpretation of the scriptures. It seems to me, though, that a literal reading is the one that does justice to these other fruitful people who have multiplied outside of the garden. There would have been plenty of women not related to Cain from whom he could have chosen his bride.

The harmonized interpretation of these scriptures might represent the beginning of the marginalization of certain segments of God's human creation. This happens again in the story of Noah and his *"household [KJV]"* who were shut up in the ark. *The LORD then said to Noah, "Go into the ark, you and your whole family, because I have found you righteous in this generation. Take with you seven of every kind of clean animal, male and its mate, and two of every kind of unclean animal, a male and its mate." (Genesis 7:1-2).* Common literature and songs would have most of us believing that Noah took two of each kind of the animals. The seven clean animals tend to be ignored. The scripture clearly states that there were seven clean males and their mates giving fourteen animals altogether.

Moreover, who was in the *"household"* of Noah? What happened to Noah's slaves? Where were the slaves who built the ark and did the work of caring for the animals and shoveling animal dung? Skilled carpenters and laborers would have been required to build the ark and surely there was much dung to be shoveled after Noah and his household were shut up inside. This would have been work for slaves, not the sons of the head of the household.

Unnamed slaves were not usually a part of Bible stories until they had a significant role to play. For example, Hagar, the slave of Abraham's wife, is not mentioned until it is time for Abraham to enter into his lustful relationship with her. *Now Sarai, Abram's wife, had borne him no children. But she had an Egyptian maidservant named Hagar; so she said to Abram, "The LORD has kept me from having children. Go, sleep with my maidservant; perhaps I can build a family through her." Abram agreed to what Sarai said. (Genesis 16:1-2).* Of course Abraham agreed. What red-blooded man would not? God, however, was not pleased with their plans because they showed a lack of trust in God. I don't know where the Egyptian, Hagar, came from, but we are told about the acquisition of some other slaves by Abraham after a near-disastrous case of mistaken identity brought on by his cowardly lie about his wife. *Then Abimelech brought sheep and cattle and male and female slaves and gave them to Abraham, and he returned Sarah his wife to him. (Genesis 20:14).* The point is that slaves were an integral part of the households of that day. Use of the more subtle *"menservants and maidservants"* cannot mask the true nature of their status as involuntary servants.

Some regard Noah and his sons as the only theologically significant people on the ark. *Then God blessed Noah and his sons, saying to them, "Be fruitful and increase in number and fill the earth. (Genesis 9:1).* The other human beings would have been participants in the fruitful multiplying that was going on but, they weren't important enough to be listed among King James' *"begats."* They were, nevertheless, part of God's creative design. My unnamed ancestors who were slaves in America applied their considerable skills to building the infrastructure of this country. Their lack of mention in many history books cannot remove the reality of their lives.

Let us go back to the fascinating story of Abraham. Abraham was a very virile man. He and Sarah laughed at God's promise that they would have children in their old age. Nevertheless, Isaac was born when Abraham was 100 years old and Sarah was 90. Yet Abraham married again after Sarah died, and had many sons by that wife. Not only that, he had concubines who bore him children as well. *Abraham took another wife, whose name was Keturah. She bore him Zimran, Jokshan, Medan, Midian, Ishbak and Shuah. Jokshan was the father of Sheba and Dedan; the descendants of Dedan were the Asshurites, the Letushites and the Leummites. The sons of Midian were Ephah, Epher, Hanoch, Abida and Eldaah. All these were descendants of Keturah. Abraham left everything he owned to Isaac. But while he was still living, he gave gifts to the sons of his concubines and sent them away from his son Isaac to the land of the east. (Genesis 25:1-6).* The inheritance went to Isaac, his favorite son, the son of Sarah his sister-wife. The sons of his concubines received some nice gifts and no inheritance before they were kicked out of the tent.

Ishmael, his son born to Hagar, was sent away while a young boy apparently with nothing but the clothes on his back, a little food and water. *And she [Sarah] said to Abraham, "Get rid of that slave woman and her son, for that slave woman's son will never share in the inheritance with my son Isaac." Early the next morning Abraham took some food and a skin of water and gave them to Hagar. He set them on her shoulders and then sent her off with the boy. She went on her way and wandered in the desert of Beersheba. (Genesis 21:10,14).* Ishmael and his mother were sent away in a most humiliating fashion. Sarah let it be known before Ishmael was born that Hagar was not her favorite person, even though she coerced Hagar into sleeping with Abraham so that she could have the child. Sarah's jealous rage caused Hagar to run away once before. This time Sarah convinced Abraham to abandon Hagar and his son. It was a permanent severance without benefits for Ishmael and his mother.

The theological reverberations of Abraham's actions are still felt to this day. The descendants of peoples who share a common genetic heritage are feuding over the legacy of this one patriarch. Many African Americans have white ancestors who took Sarah's attitude of declaring *"that slave woman's son will never share in the inheritance with my son." (Genesis 21:10)*.

There are cries in the United States today for reparations for the evil legacy of slavery. I have heard many White Americans say that they were not alive during slavery and are not personally liable for any alleged mistreatment of slaves. They may have a point on that narrow legalistic issue. They miss the point entirely, however, when considered from a biblical perspective.

The issue for me is not reparations. Reparations remind me of punitive damages in a legal proceeding. They are not the actual damages required to restore the complainant to wholeness. They are punishment ordered by the court to insure that the egregious behavior of the defendant is not repeated and that others who are similarly situated are not tempted to commit the same offense.

For me, the real issues are legacy and inheritance. My ancestors were never paid for the work they did. They, therefore, could not pass an inheritance on to me. The slaveholder's children, however, received their inheritance and lived a lifestyle that reflected it, while often claiming that they had "made it on their own," without the benefit of affirmative action and other programs designed to remedy past discrimination.

The importance of legacy can be illustrated by a common practice in colleges and universities in the United States. Major colleges and universities have for years had (mostly unwritten) admission policies called legacy admissions. The practice simply says that the children of alumni receive preferential consideration for admission. We can see a classic example of this procedure, (and its inherent flaws), in the college experience of at least one of our recent presidents.

My wife's father was born around 1898 in South Carolina. We believe that his father was a slave. My wife's grandfather, only two generations removed from her, was a slave in the United States of America! The illiteracy and poverty that were part of the slave system's legacy have affected later generations in a significant way. This is not the legacy that I aspire to possess. Give me that which was promised through Abraham: *"I will make the son of the maidservant into a nation also." (Genesis 21:11).* God promised it.

I don't want reparations or even virulent affirmative action. I want my legacy. I want the promises to be fulfilled. I want the forty acres and a mule that should have gone to my wife's grandfather. In fact, I'll take the acreage and the government can keep the mule. I want my granddaughter to have the education denied to her paternal great grandfather by a violently oppressive and racist system. I don't want reparations. I want the dollar per hour I should have earned that was paid to my white colleagues when I was making half as much. Most of all, I want to be restored to my rightful place in the heavenly family picture, covered so long by the whitewash of racist and distorted history.

My wife wants the salary she would have earned, if the company had not lied and told her that the job had just been filled—a job that was suddenly still available when she called back on the telephone.

I don't want reparations. I want my name and dignity back from telemarketers and doctors who call my home stating that this is "Dr. John Doe" and demand to speak to "Ron"—no full name, no last name, and certainly no title. I don't want reparations. I want my $1,000 back that I was charged extra for the same car that was sold to my white friends for less. I want the thousands of dollars in extra interest and closing costs paid to purchase my home. I don't want reparations. I do want refunds for the exorbitant insurance premiums paid on the ridiculously small life insurance policy (when I was allowed to buy life insurance). I don't want reparations. I want payment for service above and beyond the call of duty for thousands of young Black men killed in the prime of life while faithfully serving in the military in disproportionate numbers. I don't want reparations. I want just compensation for the widows of countless men who worked on the front lines during the industrial revolution in the face of dangerous, toxic-emitting furnaces that caused their fatal emphysema and other diseases.

I don't want reparations. I want the wealth that was stolen from me by appraisers and agents who refused to allow me to buy wherever I chose, and enforced a system that restricted some of us to sub-standard housing in racially segregated enclaves, while they enjoyed the wealth-building appreciation of their property. I want the return of my mental health stolen from me by emotional stress caused by the nooses hung on our property and the bullet fired that shattered the glass near my wife's head when we bought or sought property in the "wrong" neighborhood. I don't want reparations. I want a refund on the fine that I paid for "driving while black" through a white neighborhood.

What hope is there for the children of the slave woman? How do they overcome a forlorn tale of stolen possibilities and broken promises? *"But now, Lord, what do I look for? My hope is in you." (Psalm 39:7)* My hope is in God who keeps promises. *God heard the boy crying, and the angel of God called to Hagar from heaven and said to her, What is the matter, Hagar? Do not be afraid; God has heard the boy crying as he lies there. Lift the boy up and take him by the hand, for I will make him into a great nation. (Genesis 21:17-18).*

We have longed for the *great nation.* As with Ishmael, God heard our cry while in the desert of despair. Likewise, God fulfilled God's promise and lifted us up with the hands of Jesus Christ. *Pointing to his disciples, he said, "Here are my mother and my brothers. For whoever does the will of my Father in heaven is my brother and sister and mother." (Matthew 12:49-50).* Jesus brought the scattered nations together into one large family. He redefined family and eliminated genetic barriers and boundaries. This family, this *great nation,* is a nation for people who had been a displaced people, for people who were an oppressed people, for people who had lost their sense of identity, for people who had been slaves. Jesus was saying that when we become part of his heavenly family we have an eternal identity with God. Those who do the will of God in heaven will retrieve their family legacy and gain a rich inheritance. *And as for Ishmael, I have heard you: I will surely bless him; I will make him fruitful and will greatly increase his numbers. He will be the father of twelve rulers, and I will make him into a great nation. (Genesis 17:20).*

Chapter 15

THE "N" WORD

But who are you, O man, to talk back to God? "Shall what is formed say to him who formed it, 'Why did you make me like this?' " Does not the potter have the right to make out of the same lump of clay some pottery for noble purposes and some for common use? (Romans 9:20-21).

Dark am I, yet lovely, O daughters of Jerusalem, dark like the tents of Kedar, like the tent curtains of Solomon. Do not stare at me because I am dark, because I am darkened by the sun. My mother's sons were angry with me and made me take care of the vineyards; my own vineyard I have neglected. (Song of Solomon 1:5-6).

This is a good time to reflect on the corporate schizophrenia and paranoia that beset many of us who have African ancestry. The blues singer sang, "Lord, what did I do to be born so black and blue?" The scriptures deal with the implicit import of the question. *But who are you, O man, to talk back to God? "Shall what is formed say to him who formed it, 'Why did you make me like this?' (Romans 9:20).* The paranoia comes in part from the continuous defensive posture that many African Americans have adopted to ward off attacks from the racists who claim that we cannot possibly have a favored position with God. In fact, some have persisted in perpetuating the lie that Black people are cursed by God. It is ironic that in one of the few instances recorded in the Bible where God cursed someone by causing skin to change color, the result was that her skin became white as snow. *When the cloud lifted from above the Tent, there stood Miriam — leprous, like snow. (Numbers 12:10).*

The schizophrenia may be due to the juxtaposition of the dominant cultural pressures with the familial influences of their particular African American heritage. Ossie Davis wrote in his inimitable way of this tension, when a character in his play "Purlie Victorious," declared "Being colored can be a lot of fun when there ain't nobody looking." Even our intra-family debates about who we are and how we relate to each other have to be played out in the spotlight of the television cameras. Are we Colored or Negro or Black or African American? One person asked, "Why do you people use the 'N' word but get angry if someone else uses it?" This one for me is easy. There is a simple test that any individual can apply to decide whether he or she can use a particular word without being offensive. If you can place the word "we" before the word, you can use it. If you can't pass the "we" test, it means that you don't belong to the group in question and should avoid the use of the word.

I was reminded of this principle and sensitized to the fact that every ethnic group has special words that apply only to those inside the group by an incident that occurred in Pittsburgh almost forty years ago. My wife and I decided to go to an Italian restaurant in the East Liberty section of Pittsburgh because she loves Italian food. We went to a real Italian restaurant, not a national chain. It was small, family owned, community-based with a cozy, intimate atmosphere. We enjoyed our meal as a large Italian-American family settled in around two huge tables next to us. They were obviously having a good time and reveled in each other's company. We noticed, however, to our significant discomfort initially, that they made extensive use of a three-letter word that starts with "w" that has been applied in a pejorative way to Americans of Italian background. It was the first time that my wife and I realized that other ethnic groups have their special word too—a word that's just for them. That special "we" word only has meaning and value to those who have the right to say it.

These attitudes of schizophrenia and paranoia are also illustrated by this passage from the Bible: *"Dark am I, yet lovely, O daughters of Jerusalem, dark like the tents of Kedar..." (Song of Solomon 1:5).* It is the *"yet"* (*"but"* in the King James translation) that drives this point home. She makes the point that she is black (KJV) and that she is *lovely* or *comely* (KJV). Then, she connects these two phrases with *"but"* or *"yet"* as if one phrase stands in opposition to the other. Some scholars do suggest that *"but"* or *"yet"* may not be the best translations. They may reflect the cultural or racial bias of the translators who could not bring themselves to connect *black* and *comely* in the same sentence as positive statements inspired by God. So here we go again. She betrays a degree of paranoia: *Do not stare at me because I am dark... (Song of Solomon 1:6).* We can almost hear her voice chiming in with the blues singer, "black and blue."

God has a word for those of us of darker hues who are told that we are outside of God's plan. We especially need to reflect on this during the time that we celebrate our history. *It will happen that in the very place where it was said to them, 'You are not my people,' they will be called 'sons of the living God.'(Romans 9:26; Hosea 1:10).* America for years has said to African Americans, "You are not the people of God. You are not chosen. You are not blessed. In fact, you are cursed." But God says that in the very place where this is said, you will be called the *"sons of the living God."*

We are not the only ones to experience this name-calling. Paul was accused of being an African. *As the soldiers were about to take Paul into the barracks, he asked the commander, "May I say something to you?" "Do you speak Greek?" he replied. "Aren't you the Egyptian who started a revolt and led four thousand terrorists out into the desert some time ago?" (Acts 21:37-38).* Jesus was called a Samaritan and demon-possessed. *The Jews answered him, "Aren't we right in saying that you are a Samaritan and demon-possessed?" (John 8:48).*

As we used to say when we were children, people will call you "out of" your name. Just as Jesus and Paul were called other names, so will you and I be called the "N" word and worse. Others will use negative and obscene words and claim that they apply to you and me. Some people look at us, point toward heaven, and use the "N" word. They read the Bible and say that the Bible, when talking about us, uses the "N" word. I know what you are thinking. You are thinking that the "N" word is "Nubian," but it is not. That's right. The "N" Word is "not" or "no" or "never." The "N" word excludes rather than includes. It negates, rather than affirms. It discourages, rather than encourages.

Many of our young people don't believe they can perform on tests because of the "N" word. Even their parents tell them, "I have never been good in math." They believe "There's no way I can do it." They think, "I am not going to pass this class." The community outlook usually does not help matters because there are many "naysayers" who exude the same attitude. They surmise that "There is no way that we can turn the economy around. Employers will never bring jobs to our city. Besides, we would be the last to get the jobs if they did." The negative prospects are pervasive.

We Christians should declare "No more of this negative nonsense!" God has a word about the "N" word. "*It will happen that in the very place where it was said to them, 'You are not my people,' they will be called 'sons of the living God.'"(Romans 9:26)*. The scriptures continue to confirm God's message about name calling. *How great is the love the Father has lavished on us, that we should be called children of God! And that is what we are! The reason the world does not know us is that it did not know him.(1 John 3:1)*. While others are saying what you are not, God is saying that you are children of the living God. While others tell you what you cannot do, God says that you "*can do everything through him who gives me [you] strength. (Philippians 4:13). "* While others say that there is no way that we can solve all of the many problems that we face, God declares that God will make a way out of no way. While the world says no, you should tell your story of how God says yes.

Before I end this discourse, I must remind you that there is one "N" word given by God that is not "negative," it is not "never," it is not "no." That "N" word is a <u>name</u>.   Jesus said, "*Whatever you ask in my <u>name</u>...*" (John 14:13).   John says "*Believe in the <u>name</u> of Jesus...*" (1 John 3:23). The book of *Acts* says that "*There is no other <u>name</u> given unto men whereby they might be saved.*"(Acts 4:12). This is great news for the individual Christian, but there is also good news for that collective body of people who had the "N" word thrown at them. God says in the midst of the most troublesome times *If my people who are called by my <u>name</u> will humble themselves and pray and seek my face and turn from their wicked ways, then will I hear from heaven and will forgive their sin and will heal their land. (2 Chronicles 7:14)*. Thank God for the "N" word.

Chapter 16

"CHAPTER 10"

Then Peter began to speak: "I now realize how true it is that God does not show favoritism but accepts men from every nation who fear him and do what is right. (Acts 10:34-35).

*E*ven a jackleg preacher has some well-trained colleagues in the ministry with whom fellowship is sometimes possible. I certainly have been blessed to number some of these reverend doctors among my friends and ministerial contemporaries. They are usually very tolerant of my ignorance and wink at my obvious shortcomings in formal training. They are good friends and good friends are like that. However, suppositions in this chapter crossed the line for two of my closest and most tolerant associates.

I was presenting a seminar that considered *Luke 22:32* with special emphasis on Jesus' statement to Peter *"and when you are converted..."* (KJV). I wondered aloud "When was Peter converted? When did Peter turn back?" This question caused a surprising amount of tension; maybe outrage is a better word. The reverend doctors restrained themselves in the seminar, but cornered me at the entrance to my office, and unleashed a vigorous verbal attack on me for even asking such a preposterous question. They implied that any preacher with a modicum of Bible knowledge would know about Peter's zeal as a disciple and would not have to speculate about when he was converted. Peter was in the forefront with Christ; he performed miracles. He even received the Holy Spirit. It was obvious that Peter must have been converted well before all of this happened. The Holy Spirit surely would not fall on a man who was not converted!

Consider the record given in the book of *Acts*. In *Chapter 1* Peter speaks to the believers in the upper room to urge them to participate in fulfilling scripture by selecting a replacement for Judas. The eleven disciples selected two candidates. *Then they prayed, Lord, you know everyone's heart. Show us which of these two you have chosen to take over this apostolic ministry, which Judas left to go where he belongs. Then they cast lots...(Acts 1:24-26).* Peter, along with the disciples, prayed and asked God for guidance but turned to an ancient method of casting lots to decide on a replacement for Judas. It's in the Bible, so it must be true. However, that doesn't make Peter's actions right or approved by God.

Acts, Chapter 2 gives one of the most well-known and misunderstood accounts in all of the New Testament—the special manifestation of the Holy Spirit. Peter was present. The Holy Spirit fell on him and the others. He preached an expository sermon that explained the events to the amazed onlookers. Yet, this jackleg says, he was not converted. He had not yet experienced that ultimate change of mind that signals total surrender to the will of God.

Acts, Chapter 3 describes Peter's encounter with a man who was *"lame from birth."* Peter invoked the name of Jesus so that the man was healed and able to walk for the first time in his life. Furthermore, Peter preached another great explanatory sermon to the startled observers. Was he converted then?

Acts, Chapter 4 shows that Peter and John were thrown into jail and given a chance to explain under the guidance of the Holy Spirit, what had happened to the disabled man and to the five thousand who now believed in Jesus.

Acts, *Chapter 5* warns believers that Ananias and Sapphira were entrapped by Peter and suffered the death penalty for their deception. The apostles continued their healing ministry and persecution of the church grew.

Acts, *Chapter 6* deals with extending the administrative responsibilities of the church to followers other than the apostles. Seven men who were filled with the Holy Spirit were chosen to help the apostles manage the important secular matters that affected the members of the developing congregation.

Chapter 7 exposes the inherent physical dangers associated with establishing the early Christian church. Stephen's speech to the Sanhedrin led to his stoning as he became the first martyr for his beliefs.

Acts, *Chapter 8* points out that Peter and John were successful in invoking the Holy Spirit to enable the new believers to respond to their calls. Simon the Sorcerer was chastised for his attempts to obtain the power of the Holy Spirit through devious human means.

Acts, *Chapter 9* reports that Aeneas was healed through Peter's prayers and Dorcas was raised from the dead. Surely, Peter must have been converted by then. Or was he?

Acts, *Chapter 10* tells the story of a deeply bigoted Peter who viewed gentiles as unclean. God prepared Peter through a heavenly vision to receive Cornelius, the centurion of the Italian Regiment and other gentiles gathered at Cornelius' house. *He said to them: "You are well aware that it is against our law for a Jew to associate with a Gentile or visit him. But God has shown me that I should not call any man impure or unclean... Then Peter began to speak: "I now realize how true it is that God does not show favouritism but accepts men from every nation who fear him and do what is right. (Acts 10:28,34,35).* Peter was finally converted, that is, his mind changed from his fleshly will to obedience to the commandments of Christ.

I thank God for Simon Peter. I need to know that God used him in his sinful, unconverted state. It was not *Saint* Peter who denied Christ three times. Nor was it *Saint* Peter who spoke in unknown tongues and refused to meet with the "unclean" gentiles. It was the racist, sexist, arrogant, ignorant, vulgar, profane, dedicated, committed, compassionate, vindictive, Simon Peter who was used in a mighty way by God for nine chapters in the book of *Acts*. It was not until *Chapter 10* that he came to the realization that *"God is no respecter of persons."* *(Acts 10:34).* Have you arrived at *Chapter 10* in your life so that you can testify about God who includes all people in the heavenly vision?

Chapter 17

AMERICAN IDOL

Who has believed our message and to whom has the arm of the LORD been revealed? He grew up before him like a tender shoot, and like a root out of dry ground. He had no beauty or majesty to attract us to him, nothing in his appearance that we should desire him. (Isaiah 53:1-2).

The understandings of revelation, sin and salvation are essentially race independent or at least race neutral. However, many Christians have attached racial impressions to certain scriptures (e.g. *Genesis 9:24-27*) that re-enforce the notion that Christianity is indeed a "white man's religion." Consequently, many who are faithful members of Christian congregations find themselves nodding in agreement with some seriocomic jabs directed at the "white man's religion." These discussions force African American Christian theologians to reconsider what it means to be truly Christian and authentically black. White Christian theologians have been peculiarly silent about this point. Few of the top apologists have seriously entered this debate. Part of the reason may be that consciously or not, many white Christians do indeed regard their religion as a white man's religion. Biblical responses to refute this claim can be formulated using many scriptures such as this: *In the church at Antioch there were prophets and teachers: Barnabas, Simeon called Niger, Lucius of Cyrene, Manaen (who had been*

brought up with Herod the tetrarch) and Saul   (Acts 13:1).
Simeon called Niger and Lucius of Cyrene were clearly
African.   The African presence in the early Christian
church was documented and undeniable.

The commandment given in *Exodus 20* is probably
violated by Christians more than any other. *You shall not
make for yourself an idol in the form of anything in heaven
above or on the earth beneath or in the waters below. (Exodus
20:4)* Many Christian apologists skillfully explain away
this commandment, rationalize it or ignore it. They insist
on making images—overwhelmingly European images—
in paint, sculpture, and cinema. This is not worship, the
theologians say; this is simply representation and
therefore not an idol to be venerated. The problem is that
the image is inextricably entwined with the essence in its
presentation. God in God's wisdom directly commanded
us not to make images because God knew that we
humans could not handle them. Human beings could
not represent God visually without creating God in our
own image. Yet, when God decided to honor humans by
sending a redeemer, it was decreed that *He had no beauty
or majesty to attract us to him, nothing in his appearance that
we should desire him. (Isaiah 53:2).* Most Christian artists
chose handsome white men, often with blond hair and
blue eyes to represent Jesus. Some skilled Christian
apologists have insisted that such image-making does
not violate the second commandment and actually
honors God. These arguments notwithstanding, such
actions have indeed led to the creation of a "white man's
religion."

The impact of images portrayed by Christian
evangelists was revealed to this author by an incident
involving an eight-year-old foster child, Mark. Mark was
the resident of a highly regarded Christian institution for
children who were removed by social service agencies

from their homes. His mother was alive, but unable to care for him. My wife and I were childless at the time. We opened our home to Mark for periodic weekend visits designed to give him a glimpse of normal family life outside of the institution. Mark was a very handsome, brown-skinned African American youngster with a broad smile and even temperament. He seemed to enjoy his visits and we were delighted to have him in our home. We noticed on his first weekend that Mark liked to sit on the living room floor and rock back and forth while combing his hair. He did this with great determination and intensity. When I asked him why he did this, he answered with undisguised irritation, "Because I want to go to heaven." It took a little more prodding for Mark to explain that he had seen the pictures at the institution. He had seen Jesus, the angels, God and all the residents of heaven. He knew that none of them looked like him. His eight-year-old mind could not figure out what to do about his skin color and his nose and his eyes. But the hair, maybe, just maybe if he combed long enough, he could be accepted by God. Many white Christians have presented the god of their own creation, made in their image to Mark and millions like him. It is no mystery why so many people of color were inclined to at least listen when non-Christian groups talked about a religion that included them in the heavenly vision.

Jesus made it very clear to all of his disciples that they were to end their exclusive mission to Jews and go into all the world, Jewish and Gentile, to proclaim the good news. *Then Jesus came to them and said,... Therefore go and make disciples of all nations, baptizing them in the name of the Father and of the Son and of the Holy Spirit..."* *(Matthew 28:18-19).* Furthermore, Jesus' commandment in *Acts 1* said that the disciples were to go to all of the world and not just Jerusalem. *"But you will receive power when the Holy Spirit comes on you; and you will be my witnesses in Jerusalem, and in all Judea and Samaria, and to the ends of the earth." (Acts 1:8).* The mention of the Samaritans is especially significant. Jesus had often pointed to the Jewish interaction with the hated Samaritans to illustrate the spiritual myopia of his Jewish brothers and sisters. His love for the Samaritans gives a very compelling illustration of God's love for the descendants of those of mixed heritage, as is the case for most African Americans. Jesus knew the ancient Hebrew scripture that placed limitations on those who could worship God. *No one born of a forbidden marriage nor any of his descendants may enter the assembly of the LORD, even down to the tenth generation. (Deuteronomy 23:2).* Yet, he decreed that the Christian community includes every race and ethnic group.

The story of the Ethiopian eunuch shows that Christianity was not only racially and ethnically inclusive, but that Christ had removed the proscription of worship by emasculated or flawed men. *No one who has been emasculated by crushing or cutting may enter the assembly of the LORD. (Deuteronomy 23:1).* This representative of the queen knew that his worship was limited to an intellectual experience at a distance. It is not surprising that the eunuch chose to read this scripture from the scroll of Isaiah *(Isaiah 53)*. He surely knew what it meant to be humiliated and deprived of justice since that most important symbol of his masculinity was cruelly cut from his young body. It was by divine order that Philip was placed in the eunuch's path as he read this passage. *"In his humiliation he was deprived of justice. Who can speak of his descendants? For his life was taken from the earth." The eunuch asked Philip, "Tell me, please, who is the prophet talking about, himself or someone else?" Then Philip began with that very passage of*

Scripture and told him the good news about Jesus. As they traveled along the road, they came to some water and the eunuch said, "Look, here is water. Why shouldn't I be baptized?" (Acts 8:33-37).

The Ethiopian eunuch provided an early test of whether Christian leaders were indeed true to the teachings of the Master. Philip had to respond to the challenge: *"Look, here is water. Why shouldn't I be baptized?"* A hypocrite would have read from *Deuteronomy;* Philip baptized the man. True Christianity was now established. In opposition to those who claimed that Christianity has emasculated black men, the Bible shows that men who had been emasculated by a cruel society could come to Jesus for spiritual restoration.

Each of us must gain an empathetic understanding of the hurt that individuals such as the eunuch suffer from experiences of emasculation, an example of ostracism and disenfranchisement of innocent people. Then, we will begin to realize fully the important significance of God's commandment about creating idols. I must warn you that the following section that offers insight for persuasive obedience may outrage those who are educated in traditional conservative Christianity. Perhaps only a true Jackleg would venture into these waters.

The soldiers who carried out crucifixions broke the legs of the weakened condemned man--when they decided to end the torture--so that he could no longer push up and complete the painful process of exhaling. Have you ever wondered why the unfortunate victim of crucifixion did not just stop pushing up to exhale air and die? Why did he continue to scrape his raw skin against the rough wood of that stake? I received a possible answer from a professor in one of the two seminaries from which I received my incomplete theological education. He spoke in hushed, strained words about the dirty little secret of crucifixion as he suggested the possibility of a tactic used by the Roman executioners. They might have placed a sharp spike or stake in a strategic position so that if a man slumped and did not push up, he would develop a strong appreciation for the eunuch's excruciating pain and reverence for God's law.

The claim made by some religious groups that white people are devils who will never accept God and the racist Christian's assertion that black people are the descendants of a cursed and inferior race, are confronted by the profound truth that if we are truly in Christ, we should *"Put to death, therefore, whatever belongs to your earthly nature... which is idolatry. (Colossians 3:5).* The scripture continues to admonish that we change when we surrender the *"old self with its practices and have put on the new self, which is being renewed in knowledge in the image of its Creator. Here there is no Greek or Jew, circumcised or uncircumcised, barbarian, Scythian, slave or free, but Christ is all, and is in all." (Colossians 3:9-11).*

An ancient prophet summarizes this argument well. *Of what value is an idol, since a man has carved it? Or an image that teaches lies? (Habakkuk 2:18).* This means that true Christians must end the use of ethnically identifiable images used worship the American (or any other) idol and begin to worship God in *Spirit and in truth.*

Chapter 18

IT'S TIME TO MOVE ON!

And this will be the sign to you that it is I who have sent you: When you have brought the people out of Egypt, you will worship God on this mountain." (Exodus 3:12).

All good leaders have a measure of humility that causes them to ask, "Who am I?" Martin Luther King, Jr. was blessed in so many ways. He was extremely well educated, having earned a Ph.D. in systematic theology from one of the premier institutions in the country. He was a gifted speaker and an anointed pastor. Yet, he remained humble and lived a modest and unassuming lifestyle. He seemed, for all of his thirty-nine years, to have remained in touch with ordinary folk and to have kept his hat size at a manageable level.

Dr. King seemed so sure of his calling that he must have accepted the promise that God made to Moses and to all servants of God: *"I will be with you."* This simple but powerful assurance helps all Christians to keep the faith and proceed with boldness. You can't confront the Pharaohs of society, unless you know without any doubt that God is with you. You can confront the Montgomery jailers, if you know that God is with you. You can face the dogs and fire hoses, if you know for sure that God is with you. You can even face the specter of the lynching noose, if you know without doubt that God is with you.

Furthermore, God says that there is a simple and direct sign that God is with us: *"you will worship God on this mountain."* God called leaders to lead us to freedom for a purpose—so that we might serve God. Dr. King said that he had been to the mountaintop and given the privilege to look over into the *Promised Land*. He knew that he, personally, would not have the privilege of entering that land, but his eyes had beheld the glory of God and the fulfillment of God's promise.

We must remember that when the Israelites left Egypt, they were not simply fleeing slavery and oppression. They were not just running away from the valley of slavery and abuse. They were running to the mountaintop where they could worship God in spirit and truth. Many people forget this scripture and limit the value of the mountaintop experience. Many think that the only purpose of the mountain is to serve as a point from which one can see the *Promised Land*. They forget that God said that the mountaintop is itself a destination with a specific purpose. We don't go to the mountain so that we can look over at what God is going to do. We go to the mountain so that we can worship God in the manner that God demands. We can't worship God when we are bowing down to Pharaoh's gods. We can't worship God when all of our energy is spent trying to fend off the lashes from Pharaoh's whips. We can't worship God as slaves to someone else's demands. God says *"Tell Pharaoh to let my people go so that they might serve me!"*

Thanks to the leadership and the blood, sweat and tears of many leaders, Pharaoh finally relented and let the people of God go free. Segregation did not end, but morphed into a more subtle form. Discrimination did not cease, but became more sophisticated. The school houses were opened to all, but re-segregated by subject and curriculum. Banks would now loan to more people, but would not allow house values to appreciate in certain communities. Businesses would hire anyone, but close stores in certain communities. Congregations would welcome worshipers of all races, but 11:00 a.m. on

Sunday would still remain the most segregated hour of the week. We would all stand on the mountaintop, but we would not worship the same God. Pharaoh said that he would let them go, but chased after the people with his army and his chariots. Despite ten plagues and warnings and signs and wonders, he still could not bring himself to bow to the will of the Almighty God. Pharaoh said that he would desegregate, but he re-segregated instead. He said there would be fair, open housing. Instead, housing became so expensive in certain communities that it was open only to the most wealthy, who happened to be of mostly one race. He said no child would be left behind. Instead, some children were simply pushed ahead while others were left out.

When Pharaoh let the people go, God did not lead them on the road through the Philistine country, though that was shorter. (Exodus 13:17). God doesn't always lead us on the shortest route. Sometimes God will make us take the long way home. The long way home insures that we have all of the experiences that will serve us well when we get there. God led the people by the desert road. The desert is dry and unproductive. The desert is inhospitable, hot in the day and cold at night. We needed to learn how to take the heat and endure the cold. But we can be sure of one thing: long way or short way, God's way is the right way. *And He led them forth by the right way, That they might go to a city for a dwelling place. So, we should give thanks to God for leading us. (Psalm 107:7 NKJV).*

We were not of one mind about how to obtain our freedom. One group preferred slavery in Egypt, to the uncertainty of the wilderness. That is, some people said we should wait and all try to get along. Racists are basically good people who will eventually grant us our rights, by and by. One day they will voluntarily relinquish or share power. The second group was satisfied to stop wherever they were at the end of the day and gather manna from heaven for sustenance. This group said, "We have made some progress. Don't push too hard. Some of us have jobs we never got before. We can work in the downtown department stores. We can eat in most of the restaurants now and go to some movie theaters and buy the Cadillac of our choice. That's enough. Take it slow."

Moses and a small group of his closest allies wanted to move on. *Then the LORD said to Moses, "Why are you crying out to me? Tell the Israelites to move on."* *(Exodus 14:15)*. This was not a criticism, but an encouragement. Trust God and move on. Move on toward the goal that God has set for you. Move on to the place where you can truly worship God. So many people are still asking, "How long Lord? How long?" I hear God answering, *"Why are you crying out to me? Move on!"* Move on to reach the goal I have set for you. Trust God and move on. Paul expressed it so well in *Philippians 3:12-14. I press on to take hold of that for which Christ Jesus took hold of me. Brothers, I do not consider myself yet to have taken hold of it. But one thing I do know: Forgetting what is behind and straining toward what is ahead, I press on toward the goal to win the prize for which God has called me heavenward in Christ Jesus.*

THEOLOGY

In its simplest sense theology means the study of God and God's relationship to the universe. In a real way, this entire book is about God and therefore deals with theology. However, if one takes a narrower view, the next six chapters examine the character and actions of God in a way that allows us to form a relationship with God that can lead to more godly behavior.

Chapter 19

SAME OLD, SAME OLD

What has been will be again, what has been done will be done again; there is nothing new under the sun. Is there anything of which one can say, "Look! This is something new?" It was here already, long ago; it was here before our time. (Ecclesiastes 1:9-10).

Ask some people how things are going and they will give you a weary look and answer, "same old, same old." Life for them is a rut of unproductive sameness. Nothing seems to change. Nothing gets better; nothing gets worse. This means that we have to look forward to more of the same old, same old in each new year. It sounds really boring when it is said like that. Not only that, but God already knows all about me; God knows everything that I am thinking, saying or doing. The psalmist says, *Before a word is on my tongue you know it completely, O Lord. You hem me in--behind and before; you have laid your hand upon me. (Psalm 139:4-5).* This is what the theologians call predestination because God has already determined everything. It's going to be the same old, same old. The writer of *Ecclesiastes* summed up the same idea: *"What has been will be again, what has been done will be done again; there is nothing new under the sun." (Ecclesiastes 1:9).*

Some people were excited about Jesus because they thought that he had come to change the old into the new. After all, they were tired of the same old, same old and longed for a new day. Imagine their shock and disappointment when Jesus said in his Sermon on the

Mount, *"Do not think that I have come to abolish the Law or the Prophets; I have not come to abolish them but to fulfill them." (Matthew 5:17).* Jesus came to fulfill and accomplish, not to abolish. Simon, the Zealot, had difficulty believing this. Judas Iscariot could not accept it. They were tired of the same old thing. They were fed up with cruel Roman rule. It was time for a change. Their dissatisfaction with the status quo led them to believe that Jesus was the one to bring about the change in spite of what he said. F. F. Bruce in *The Hard Sayings of Jesus* writes that, "The Law for Jesus was the expression of God's will. The will of God is eternal and unchangeable. Jesus did not come to modify the will of God; he fulfilled it." Paul even writes about the fulfillment of the Law in us: *For what the law was powerless to do in that it was weakened by the sinful nature, God did by sending his own Son in the likeness of sinful man to be a sin offering. And so he condemned sin in sinful man, in order that the righteous requirements of the Law might be fully met [fulfilled] in us, who do not live according to the sinful nature but according to the Spirit. (Romans 8:3-4).*

We recall that Jesus' most famous encounter with John the Baptist--the occasion of his baptism by John-- was intricately related to the need to fulfill the requirements of the Law. John uttered an understandable protest against Jesus' request for baptism. First of all, John knew that baptism was understood as a sign of repentance for sins. Jesus had not sinned and clearly did not need baptism for that purpose. Jesus' answer indicated his single-minded intent to fulfill the Law: *Then Jesus came from Galilee to the Jordan to be baptized by John. But John tried to deter him, saying, "I need to be baptized by you, and do you come to me?" Jesus replied, "Let it be so now; it is proper for us to do this to fulfill all righteousness." Then John consented. (Matthew 3:13-15).* Jesus, through John's baptism, identified fully with sinful human beings by symbolically taking upon himself their sins as if they were his own. He would eventually give this vicarious representation its ultimate expression on the cross.

The people in the synagogue, a place for worship and instruction, thought that everything was the same old, same old. Rabbis came and went and expounded in the same old way until a rabbi named Jesus came along. I am sure that the word must have spread that this man was saying something brand new and very strange. *John records a portion of one very troubling and unsettling sermon: I am the living bread that came down from heaven. If anyone eats of this bread, he will live forever." (John 6:51).* There was strong opposition to what Jesus said. *Then the Jews began to argue sharply among themselves, "How can this man give us his flesh to eat?"(John6:52).* Jesus reacted to their incredulity with an even more outrageous reiteration of his point that carried it even further. *Jesus said to them, "I tell you the truth, unless you eat the flesh of the Son of Man and drink his blood, you have no life in you. (John 6:53).* The implication was that those who refuse to accept, embrace, profess and practice his teachings are spiritually dead.

It was the grumbling of the disciples that really concerned Jesus. It was their offense that bothered him most. He did not expect the Pharisees and other religious leaders to understand. They were too busy ridiculing this theological heresy to entertain the possibility of its truth. But the disciples needed to grasp the deep insightful revelation inherent in Jesus' words. That's why Jesus continued the discourse with the disciples. *Aware that his disciples were grumbling about this, Jesus said to them, "Does this offend you? What if you see the Son of Man ascend to where he was before! The Spirit gives life; the flesh counts for nothing. The words I have spoken to you are spirit and they are life. (John 6:61-63).* In other words, Jesus was asking his disciples if they had to observe once again the miraculous and the supernatural, in order to believe. Did they need to see him ascend again to the one he called Father? The challenge was for them to consider what it would take for them to believe, since they could not accept the words of Jesus.

Beyond all of this, however, was Jesus' desire to have the disciples move their level of understanding from the earthly to the celestial. They thought about food in terms of physical digestion instead of spiritual assimilation. Jesus explained that it was not about his flesh. He was not talking about food in the literal, physical sense. Rather, the ingestion of his words, the belief in his divine heritage and ultimately his selfless sacrifice, will lead to the fullness of life, temporal and everlasting. Jesus further admonished his disciples, *"Yet there are some of you who do not believe." (John 6:64).* He did not expect belief from his critics. He craved it from his devout followers.

The Last Supper was just the same old, same old-- the same prayers, the same songs, the same food--until Jesus repeated what he had taught in the synagogue that offended some disciples and Pharisees months earlier. Jesus had taught, *"I am the bread of life...the bread that comes down from heaven, which a man may eat and not die... This bread is my flesh, which I will give for the life of the world." (John 6:48-51).* The disciples were hearing it once more *"This is my body." (Mark 14:22) This is my blood."* *(Mark 14:24).* The disciples present that night must have been stunned. They thought this foolishness had been put to rest months ago. Surely Jesus knew that this was a *"hard saying"* that offended some believers so much that they left him. He, himself, had acknowledged that they were the ones who had remained with him through his trials.   Yet, when the traditional meal had ended, he resurrected this strange notion of spiritual cannibalism.

Jesus was determined that these last faithful disciples come to understand who he was and why he came. He was just a few hours away from his agonizing and torturously humiliating death on a Roman cross. He could see beyond the cross, but they could not; they would not unless they understood that the "bread of heaven" must be consumed in order for them to have spiritual life. He was not being facetious when he spoke in the synagogue and he was deadly serious now.

Furthermore, he told these disciples to make a habit of eating this special meal in this way in his memory. Jesus knew the ancient word. *There is no remembrance of men of old, and even those who are yet to come will not be remembered by those who follow. (Ecclesiastes 1:11).* He wanted these closest disciples to remember that he is the bread of life. His body and his blood provide the spiritual sacrifice that completely fulfills the requirements of the Law. If they forget Jesus and his words which had been so difficult for them to receive, they will not be able to enter into that eternal life that can only be attained through and with Jesus. His request that they remember him can best be understood within the context of this last meal that Jesus shared before his death. This meal was the actualization of his teaching in the synagogue about the spiritual consumption of the bread of life.

The memories of Jesus should not be just that of his pain, but should include the joy and hope that Jesus brought through his suffering. Part of what he was talking about was remembering the joy. Jesus' desire, I am convinced, was that those who believe in him would be able to sing his praises loudly.   "I remember, Jesus, how I was able to lean on you when I sat around the table. I remember the joy that I felt. I remember how we celebrated and we were so excited when the Holy Spirit came upon us in a fresh way. I remember the love that you showed to everybody, including me. I remember the compassion that you showed." When you think about Jesus as you celebrate Holy Communion, realize that he was saying that we must remember the triumphant Jesus who overcame death. Remember the time when he called Lazarus forth from the grave. Remember the one who said *all power is in my hand.* Remember the one who gave the commission and the charge to go into *all the world.* Remember this joyful, triumphant Jesus every time you share in this meal with your Christian brothers and sisters.

Jesus' mission to fulfill the Law might offer the best explanation of why Jesus was determined to return to Jerusalem and the cross for one last time. *Hebrews* quotes the prophetic words of *Psalm 40* to show the driving motivation toward ultimate fulfillment of the Law as lived out by Jesus: *Then I said, 'Here I am--it is written about me in the scroll--I have come to do your will, O God.' First, he said, "Sacrifices and offerings, burnt offerings and sin offerings you did not desire, nor were you pleased with them" (although the Law required them to be made). (Hebrews 10:7-9).* Let us not go about the same old business of forgetfulness where there is no remembrance of our Bread of Life. Jesus became the perfect sacrifice who could cry from the cross, *"It is finished!"*

Chapter 20

THE THEOLOGY OF THE SMALL

For you created my inmost being; you knit me together in my mother's womb. I praise you because I am fearfully and wonderfully made. (Psalm 139:13-14).

God is great. The youngest child knows this attribute of God. God is so big, so vast in scope, so pervasive that our minds cannot encompass God. We know from science that even the vastness of space cannot place boundaries on the greatness of God. Then, it is not surprising that we think of God in the realm of the LARGE: "So high that we can't get over Him, so low that we can't get under Him, so wide that we can't go around Him." I certainly will not mount a challenge to this idea. However, the true greatness of God can only be apprehended when we appreciate the theology of the small.

Some scientists propose that species evolve and adapt in response to environmental influences. They suggest that these changes occur in a way that the ability of the organism to survive is enhanced. It is easy to understand why many have been seduced by these arguments. Many theologians have conceded this battle to the evolutionists and proponents of natural selection and survival of the fittest. This unfortunate capitulation on the part of the religious may be due to their failure to understand the theology of the small.

The first evolutionist was probably Aaron, the brother of Moses. Moses demanded that Aaron explain how he could have allowed the people to create and worship a golden calf. Aaron gave an answer that parallels the evolutionist's explanation about the origin of the species--it just happened. *I told them, 'Whoever has any gold jewelry, take it off.' Then they gave me the gold, and I threw it into the fire, and out came this calf!"* (Exodus 32:24). Aaron's answer was incredible. First, he said that it was the fault of the people. Not bad, Aaron. Many spiritual leaders today blame the people for their fall into apostasy. The second part of his excuse was even more ridiculous. It wasn't his fault because a most amazing thing happened. He threw the gold into the fire and the golden idol just came out! Many Christians today become idol worshipers in the same way. It wasn't their fault. It wasn't intentional. They just threw the gold into the fire, and the idol came out.

One of my professors in seminary used to ask the class who had found any nuggets in the scripture. He said that a nugget was a special truth about God revealed through our studies and meditation. In other words, this knowledge of God was like pure gold. So many of us take the golden nuggets of biblical truth and cast them into the fires of doubt, prejudice, racism, gender bias and, exploitation. Then, we put the idols in God's place. We become so engrossed in our idol worshipping that we declare, "I don't know where those idols came from." Sometimes we won't acknowledge that they exist. When God reminds us through the Word that we were told not to make any *"graven images,"* we say that we just cast the golden nuggets into the fire, and the image came out.

Let me remind those who deny God's existence that it is in the realm of the small that the existence and greatness of God are truly shown. Instructions encoded in microscopic DNA determine the behavior and appearance of an organism in the macroscopic world. Nothing that happens in the world of the LARGE can convince the molecular actors that they should structure

and deport themselves differently. The logic and design
evident in these minute configurations cry out as a most
elegant testament of the handiwork of God. That
evidence is everywhere, omnipresent in tiny entities
apprehensible through the theology of the small.

The phrase "quantum leap" has entered the
language as an indication of a major transition. The
quantum, in fact, is a small fundamental unit of energy.
Quantum changes are not gradual, slowly changing
steps, but abrupt transitions from one state of being to
another. Though not large, they are quick and complete.
God is in the business of making quantum leaps. This is
evident by the zygotic entity formed during human
reproduction as sanctioned by God *(Genesis 1:27-28)*.
This process requires a definite amount of energy to
bring about an abrupt change, transforming microscopic
male and female reproductive cells into another state--an
embryo that becomes a fetus and finally, a fully
developed baby. The small includes even the fetus.
Some choose to call it something other than life. Some
depersonalize it and treat it as if it evolved haphazardly
by throwing something into the fire to bring it into
existence. This is far from the truth! The fetus clearly fits
into the divine realm of the small as one of God's
magnificent designs.

In light of all of this, we need to reconsider the
possibilities about how God interacts with humans.
Jesus often told his disciples that the kingdom of God is
within. (Luke 17:21). If one allows the possibility that he
meant that literally, it places the kingdom rule in the area
of the small. The implication of this possibility causes
discomfort in some and outrage in others. If the
kingdom of heaven is the place where God rules, then
God rules in a very small place. God's decision to give
me brown eyes was made in a microscopic strand of

DNA. It was not an evolutionary response to macroscopic stimuli or conditions. Neither did it *"just happen."* God decreed that it would be so as a natural consequence of God's creative design. I can see and know that I see through the unbelievably complex interactions of rods, cones, neurons and a multitude of other entities. God makes decisions in the place where God rules and invokes the theological precepts of the kingdom of the small within to declare to observers in the world of the LARGE that God is at work! The psalmist expressed it well. *For you created my inmost being; you knit me together in my mother's womb. I praise you because I am fearfully and wonderfully made. (Psalm 139:14).*

What are we to make of this when we consider that we have always been told about the vastness of God? God is infinite in power, wisdom, love, and dominion. We need to be reminded that the infinitesimal is part of the infinite. A significant part of God's amazing creative process occurs in the sub-microscopic world of atoms, molecules, electrons and protons. God's reign in the kingdom of the small shows how truly awesome God is.

Chapter 21

UNFORGIVABLE

They came to Capernaum. When he was in the house, he asked them, "What were you arguing about on the road?" But they kept quiet because on the way they had argued about who was the greatest. Sitting down, Jesus called the Twelve and said, "If anyone wants to be first, he must be the very last, and the servant of all." (Mark 9:33-35).

Palm Sunday is the day when we celebrate the triumphal entry of Jesus into Jerusalem for the last time. We recall the people who lined each side of the road and cried "Hosanna". We continue the celebration by distributing and blessing palms. I wonder, though, if we realize that the true significance of that day can only be understood if we consider the preparation for that last trip. We have to go back to the place where the journey began.

The trip did not begin well. Jesus inquired about the conversations of the disciples. He was concerned about their words that indicated their state of mind. *He asked them, "What were you arguing about on the road?" But they kept quiet because on the way they had argued about who was the greatest. Sitting down, Jesus called the Twelve and said, "If anyone wants to be first, he must be the very last, and the servant of all." (Mark 9:33-35).* It is clear that Jesus' disciples did not understand the nature of the kingdom that he was ushering in. They wanted places of honor in his kingdom on his right hand and his left as they argued and jockeyed for positions of honor even during these critical final moments of the ministry in the northern

126

regions. That's why Jesus tried to reason with his stubborn disciples by explaining that the one who would be first must be willing to accept a humble place.

Another incident makes it clear that their ego-dulled minds still did not get the point. *"Teacher," said John, "we saw a man driving out demons in your name and we told him to stop, because he was not one of us." (Mark 9:38-39).* The disciples felt that they belonged to an exclusive organization with special places of privilege. They were not happy about anyone infringing on their copyright. They put a quick stop to the usurper's activities but still felt a surprising need to tell Jesus. He rebuked them for a somewhat cryptic reason related to what the person might say. Once again, he pointed to the importance of words. *"Do not stop him," Jesus said. "No one who does a miracle in my name can in the next moment say anything bad about me, for whoever is not against us is for us." (Mark 9:39-40).*

They finally started on their way to Jerusalem as they had done several times before. There were subtle but significant differences this time. First, Jesus, who was normally very social, walked at the head of the convoy by himself. This change in behavior to this isolationist leadership role was unsettling for the Apostles and the other disciples who were part of the entourage. *They were on their way up to Jerusalem, with Jesus leading the way, and the disciples were astonished, while those who followed were afraid. (Mark 10:32).* The disciples were astonished that Jesus ignored their words of warning and burst to the fore to lead this tragic parade. The other followers were afraid and confused by their Master's determination to leave the fellowship of family and friends and travel once again to an uncertain fate in Jerusalem.

Jesus understood the puzzlement of his twelve close disciples. That's why he took them aside to explain to them all that was about to occur. *Again he took the Twelve aside and told them what was going to happen to him. (Mark 10:32).* His explanation must have been very unsettling indeed. These were men who were hoping for positions of power and influence in the coming kingdom who now heard their king describe the ignominious fate awaiting him and possibly awaiting them also. His first word was about betrayal. *"We are going up to Jerusalem,"* he said, *"and the Son of Man will be betrayed to the chief priests and teachers of the law. (Mark 10:33).* This must have made some disciples very nervous and anxious.

Jesus pressed on with even more disturbing words. *They will condemn him to death and will hand him over to the Gentiles, (Mark 10:33).* They understood well what it meant to be condemned. Condemnation meant that a person no longer could hope for mercy. The sentence was harsh with no possibility of leniency. These disciples had shown that they could be a little slow to perceive the truth so Jesus broke it down for them into the distressing details. He told them that the Gentiles *will mock him and spit on him, flog him and kill him. (Mark 10:34).*

The order of this list is compellingly revealing. Mocking, an act committed with the mouth, would be the first part of this excruciating suffering that Jesus was to bear. It is one of the most painful sources of human suffering even in modern times. The disciples were arguing about greatness yet one of them would whisper words of betrayal. Jesus had rebuked them for stopping someone from calling his name because Jesus said they would not *say* anything bad about him; that is, they would not mock him. He showed concern about what people were saying about him from the early days of his ministry. He asked his disciples one day, *"Who do people say that I am?"(Mark 8:27).*

Jesus had often tried to show the disciples the importance of words. The miracle that led to his chilling words about the one act that is beyond the possibility of forgiveness grew out of an encounter with a man who was blind and mute. The decision to perform this miracle was surely related to Jesus' need to teach the disciples another lesson about the power of the spoken word for good or evil. *Then they brought him a demon-possessed man who was blind and mute, and Jesus healed him, so that he could both talk and see. All the people were astonished and said, "Could this be the Son of David? But when the Pharisees heard this, they said, "It is only by Beelzebub, the prince of demons, that this fellow drives out demons." (Matthew 12:22-24).* It was Jesus' reaction to these words that led to his declaration that there is one sin so egregious and heinous that it is beyond the possibility of forgiveness, even by a God who is love. *And so I tell you, every sin and blasphemy will be forgiven men, but the blasphemy against the Spirit will not be forgiven. Anyone who speaks a word against the Son of Man will be forgiven, but anyone who speaks against the Holy Spirit will not be forgiven, either in this age or in the age to come. (Matthew 12:31-32).*

The scripture above makes Jesus' concern about the words spoken by the disciples more understandable. He knew that words were the only things that could possibly separate them from his love. He had warned them in earlier teachings that words gave audible expression to the sentiments harbored within the heart. Evil words indicate an evil heart and mind. Moreover, those same words will provide the basis for the ultimate judgment that every person must eventually face. That's why he threw strong words to the religious leaders, *You brood of vipers, how can you who are evil say anything good?*

For out of the overflow of the heart the mouth speaks. The good man brings good things out of the good stored up in him, and the evil man brings evil things out of the evil stored up in him. But I tell you that men will have to give account on the day of judgment for every careless word they have spoken. For by your words you will be acquitted, and by your words you will be condemned." (Matthew 12:34-37).

Jesus was always preparing his disciples for his final return to Jerusalem. Each opportunity that he received during his travel pointed in the direction of the cross and the resurrection. Even though Jesus reminded the disciples of the agony that he would endure before he reached the end of his earthly journey, he had presented them with marvelous words of hope along the way. These words were probably not fully understood by the disciples but they must have brought the only element of relief in this classroom session. *Three days later he will rise."* (Mark 10:34). What a glorious lesson on the road to Jerusalem!

Chapter 22

RECEIVE THE HOLY SPIRIT

Again Jesus said, "Peace be with you! As the Father has sent me, I am sending you." And with that he breathed on them and said, "Receive the Holy Spirit." (John 20:21-22).

The Holy Spirit is the third person in the Trinity. This means that the Holy Spirit has personality and will. Many of us pray to the Father or to the Son, but not to the Holy Spirit. Furthermore, the artists painted pictures of God the Father and Jesus, so that we could know what they look like. Therefore, when we pray, we have the benefit of a mental image of who God is. We know that God the Father is a big, old white man with a long beard and a finger outstretched to touch the man that he created. Jesus is blond-haired, blue-eyed with pale skin. If we ever forget what Jesus looks like, we can look at the pictures hanging on the walls of our churches to refresh our memories.

The Holy Spirit, however, presents a problem. We don't have any good portraits of the Holy Spirit. The Holy Spirit apparently did not sit still long enough for the artists to do their work. Doves and tongues of fire do appear in some paintings, but even the most literal of us realize that those are figurative representations of the Holy Spirit and should not be taken seriously like those pictures of Jesus and God the Father. It is as if the Holy Spirit does not have a personality and is not really, truly God.

When Jesus said he was going to return to the place from which he was sent, he promised not to leave the disciples alone. He said he would send a comforter to them. This is one of the most misunderstood scriptures because some people take this to mean that the Holy Spirit wasn't around all along, as if the Holy Spirit suddenly came into being or was raised from inactivity.

Almost sixty years ago, my father was in the military. He had been drafted into the Army during World War II. He came out of World War II, went to college and then into Officers Candidates School (OCS). He became a Lieutenant during the time of the Korean War. Half of his class at OCS was sent to Korea, where I'm sorry to say, most of them died as Lieutenants on the battlefield. My father was in the Chemical Corp assigned to go to Great Britain. He stood on the back porch with my mother and their three young children as he prepared to leave for his three-year tour of duty. We would join him later and spend two and a half years with him. As he was ready to leave he said to us, "Don't be so sad. I'm not leaving you alone. Your mother is with you." He was leaving us with our mother who would take care of us and comfort us. She didn't suddenly come into existence. She didn't suddenly appear on the scene just because he was going away. She was there all along.

Likewise, the Holy Spirit didn't suddenly come into existence. Jesus was telling the disciples that they had another Comforter who was with him from eternity past. Most Christians will tell you with great confidence that they know when the Holy Spirit came upon the disciples. They quickly point to the second chapter of the *Book of Acts*. However, there were actually at least three special manifestations of the power of the Holy Spirit.

The first is recorded in John's Gospel when Jesus appeared to his disciples after the resurrection. *Again Jesus said, "Peace be with you! As the Father has sent me, I am sending you." And with that he breathed on them and said,*

"Receive the Holy Spirit." (John 20:21-22). This meant that the ten apostles (Thomas was absent) received the Holy Spirit right then. Some people are so fixated on the Pentecost event that they deny that the Apostles received the Holy Spirit at this time. Maybe Jesus was just preparing them for the later event, they suggest. I believe, however, that the Bible is true. When Jesus said, *"It is finished,"* it was finished, not almost done. When Jesus declared, *"Your daughter is healed,"* she was healed instantly and completely. She wasn't about to be healed one day, by and by. Therefore, when Jesus said, *"Receive the Holy Spirit,"* they received. This means that before the day of Pentecost, there were at least ten apostles from Galilee who had already been filled with the Holy Spirit by this encounter with the risen Lord Jesus.

The well-known Pentecost experience of *Acts 2* is actually the second time that the disciples had a special encounter with the Holy Spirit. It is the one that has so captured the imagination of the Church that many people think that it was the only such experience or at least the unchangeable prototype for the action of the Holy Spirit.

The purpose of Pentecost was for the disciples to receive the power to do what God had called them to do. In order to do that, they needed the ability to communicate with people from many nations and cultures. That is, they needed to be able to speak many languages that they did not know. When the Holy Spirit came upon them, the disciples were able to speak in such a way that many of those gathered were amazed. In other words, not everybody who witnessed this experience spoke. In fact, the only ones who were doing the special speaking were Galileans. *Utterly amazed, they asked: "Are not all these men who are speaking Galileans? Then how is it that each of us hears them in his own native language?" (Acts 2:7-8).* When the disciples spoke under the power of the Holy Spirit, it didn't sound like gibberish. The people could hear and understand in their own language what God was saying to them.

There are people today who will tell you that this amazing ability to "speak in tongues" is the key evidence of salvation. The Bible says that *"When the day of Pentecost came they were all together in one place... They saw what seemed to be tongues of fire that separated and came to rest on each of them. All of them were filled with the Holy Spirit and began to speak in other tongues as the Spirit enabled them." (Acts 2:1-4).* Do you know who *"they"* were? They were the Apostles, followers of Christ. Do you know what their salvation status was? They were already saved.

The third time that the Holy Spirit showed up in a special way was days after the Pentecost event. Two leaders of the church had been imprisoned because of their direct and cutting preaching. God came through and miraculously released them so that they could return to the church. The whole church went into prayer to God. *On their release, Peter and John went back to their own people and reported all that the chief priests and elders had said to them. Now, Lord, consider their threats and enable your servants to speak your word with great boldness. Stretch out your hand to heal and perform miraculous signs and wonders through the name of your holy servant Jesus. After they prayed, the place where they were meeting was shaken. And they were all filled with the Holy Spirit and spoke the word of God boldly. (Acts 4:23,29-31).*

They prayed that God would give them the courage to preach the word *boldly!* The Holy Spirit is in the business of answering the prayers of the faithful and giving them the power to overcome evil and carry out the will of God. God took away the fear so that Peter and

John could stand up in the face of the devil, stand up in the midst of danger, and tell a dying world that there is a Savior.

Consider Paul's final prayer in the Epistle to the Ephesians. He did not pray for freedom. He did not pray for wealth. He did not even pray for health. He prayed that he might preach fearlessly (boldly). *Pray also for me, that whenever I open my mouth, words may be given me so that I will fearlessly make known the mystery of the gospel, for which I am an ambassador in chains. Pray that I may declare it fearlessly, as I should. (Ephesians 6:19-20).* The Apostle's prayer is the same as that of the early church described in the fourth chapter of *Acts.* Paul in essence prayed for the Holy Spirit to descend upon him so that he was able to carry out God's work with *boldness.* This should be the desire of any Christian who seeks to do God's will.

Because God, the Holy Spirit, is always with us we have the power to witness even to the ends of the earth. *But you will receive power when the Holy Spirit comes on you; and you will be my witness in Jerusalem and in all Judea and Samaria, and to the ends of the earth. (Acts 1:8).* Paul reminded Timothy of this in his letter of encouragement to continue his sincere, faithful service in spreading the gospel. *For this reason I remind you to fan into flame the gift of God, which is in you through the laying on of my hands. For God did not give us a spirit of timidity, but a spirit of power, of love and self-discipline. (Timothy 1:6-7).* We must prepare ourselves to receive the gift of the Holy Spirit so that we can boldly communicate God's message to people of every nation, language, and culture.

Chapter 23

AN EMPTY FEELING

If you have any encouragement from being united with Christ, if any comfort from his love, if any fellowship with the Spirit, if any tenderness and compassion, then make my joy complete by being like-minded, having the same love, being one in spirit and purpose. Do nothing out of selfish ambition or vain conceit, but in humility consider others better than yourselves. Each of you should look not only to your own interests, but also to the interests of others. Your attitude should be the same as that of Christ Jesus. (Philippians 2:1-5).

The Authorized Version uses the well-known expression, *Let this mind be in you, which was also in Christ Jesus.* We need to think about life in the same way that Jesus thought when he was on earth in the flesh. What was this attitude of Christ? First, it was an attitude of humility. This is saying a lot. Most of us are very interested in recognition, status, and having others defer to us. We want plaques to hang on the wall and certificates of merit. We want the highest grade and, of course, all of our children are well above average. Christ was meek and lowly. *Who, being in very nature God, did not consider equality with God something to be grasped, but made himself nothing. (Philippians 2:6).*

This is one of the most difficult and debated scriptures in the entire Bible. The Greek word for what Jesus did is *ekenosen*; it is active, not passive. This was not something that was done to Jesus. Jesus did it. He "*emptied himself.*" Some theologians get nervous and uncomfortable with this translation. They argue that

Jesus was always God and remained fully God throughout his incarnation. I believe that they are correct. However, God, who is sovereign, can define the Godly characteristics during any phase of God's existence. Jesus, as the agent of creation in eternity past, had all of these characteristics and more. I believe that this view is neither frightening nor heretical. It is in fact the highest expression of the love of God. His love was so great that he voluntarily set aside these divine characteristics and entrusted them to the one whom he called Father. He could ask for them at any time through prayer, but he could not invoke them on his own. To say that God *"gave his son"* means that all persons of the Trinity were full participants in the process of giving. Thus, Christ "gave" himself. He did it, in part, through this kenosis or emptying of himself.

Consider all of the characteristics of God: omnipresence, omniscience, and omnipotence. Omnipresence means the ability to be everywhere at once. God is like that. But Jesus chose to take a human body, which could only be in one place at a time. He voluntarily set aside this Godly characteristic when he chose to take on a human body. If he had remained omnipresent he would not have been confined to the cross, since only a minute part of his being would have been nailed to that stake while he was omnipresent throughout the rest of creation.

Omniscience means all knowing or all wise. The fact is that Jesus himself said that there were some things that he did not know. Only the Father knew them. Before you send me nasty text messages and accuse me of blasphemy, consider *Mark's* declaration: *No one knows about that day or hour, not even the angels in heaven, nor the Son, but only the Father. (Mark 13:32).* It seems pretty

clear to me.   Even the Son didn't know certain things
while he was on earth in his human form.

Omnipotence means that God has all power. The
Triune God has and always had all power. Therefore,
the pre-incarnate Christ had all power. In what ways did
Jesus limit his power?   He relinquished his share of
power and took *the very nature of a servant being made in
human likeness. (Philip. 2:7).*   Many of the most
conservative biblical exegetes are greatly disturbed by
these ideas. They take great offense at the notion that
Jesus' divinity was in any way limited or restricted by his
humanness. They might be surprised to know that I
share with them a zealous high regard for the
unmitigated divinity and sovereignty of Christ.   That
sovereignty, however, includes God's ability to become
manifest in whatever form pleases God, including a
human body that is subject to the space-time constraints
that the non-incarnate God transcends. His complete
transformation showed that the relinquishing of his
highest attributes was complete. This notion was so
difficult for the apostles to grasp that Jesus had to
demonstrate his status and his commandment by
washing their feet. *And being found in appearance as a man,
he humbled himself and became obedient to death--even death
on a cross! (Philip. 2:8).*

This is why we celebrate the Resurrection Sunday
called Easter. Christmas is a wonderful holiday. I
especially enjoy the time with family and friends. But
Christmas without Easter would be an empty time of
crass consumerism.   If he had not gone about his
Father's business, if he had resisted the Holy Spirit that
rested and remained on him, if he had not become
obedient to death on a cross, we would have nothing to
celebrate on Easter morning. *Therefore God exalted him to
the highest place and gave him the name that is above every*

name, that at the name of Jesus every knee should bow, in heaven and on earth and under the earth, and every tongue confess that Jesus Christ is Lord, to the glory of God the Father. (Philip. 2:9,10).

Because he was obedient to the plan that he had developed in eternity past with the Father and the Holy Spirit, he was given a name above all names. That obedience came from one who limited himself to the same constraints that we experience. We cannot claim the excuse of human limitations as we cop a plea for our sinful failures. Jesus proved that the power of God transcends human limitations if we are obedient to God and empowered by the Holy Spirit.

Many of us have never truly understood the idea that he died for us. After all, if he kept control over all of his divine attributes, he was not truly experiencing what a real man would experience. Merely feeling physical pain, no matter how agonizing would not have been enough. Many men and women have experienced even more intense pain than that suffered by Jesus. If he had known that he could of his own volition come down off of the cross and end his agony, it would have diminished the effect of his passion. Moreover, if there had been no risk, if he had just been pretending to depend on the Father and the Holy Spirit while remaining in control of his divine attributes, he would have endured nothing but a finite measure of physical pain.

That's why I can sing with my ancestors, "Sometimes it causes me to tremble" when I think about what Jesus risked. He put eternity on the line for us. If he had failed, not only would we still be lost in our sins; he would have lost eternity. Don't profane and demean the sacrifice of our savior with bunnies and eggs. Let us honor him by committing our lives to humble service. Thank him for enduring that empty feeling that lasted until his post-resurrection declaration, *"All authority in heaven and on earth has been given to me." (Matthew 28:18).* He gave it up and now he had it back. He completed his mission, reclaimed his eternally divine heritage and resumed his rightful position of authority with the Father and the Holy Spirit.

Chapter 24

THIS WELL IS DEEP

"For my thoughts are not your thoughts, neither are your ways my ways," declares the Lord. "As the heavens are higher than the earth, so are my ways higher than your ways and my thoughts than your thoughts." (Isaiah 55:8-9).

This book cannot end until we have dealt with the deepest, most troubling of all of *the deep things*. We touched on it in chapters 3 and 5. It concerns pain, torture, punishment, hell, heaven, and divine love. Why is there so much pain? Pain, when properly used, is an important part of God's design. When our human reticence to act causes us to hesitate when we need to seek medical attention, God gives us the gift of pain. Pain is insistent. Some other sensation could be put off or delayed. Human beings, however, inflict pain through torture and abuse. At least an incremental capacity for evil is a necessary characteristic of human beings. Without it we wouldn't be human. Indifference would make us mere animals; joy in it would make us demons; absence would make us divine.

Human suffering is difficult to explain under any circumstances. We want to cry out to God but we have been taught that one does not question God. So we suffer in silence. Yet the silence does not end the agonizing questions. Why does God not answer when the righteous cry for deliverance from evil? Why were people who claimed to know God skinned alive, burned at the stake, crucified and murdered by the millions? Why were innocent little children mutilated and abused with no apparent response from a just God? Ancient prophets asked the same questions. *How long, O Lord, must I call for help, but you do not listen? Or cry out to you, "Violence!" but you do not save? (Habakkuk 1:2).*

Some suggest that God did not act because God did not want to get involved. Did God do the work of creation and then withdraw to another realm unconcerned about the fate of the creation or, as others say, is God powerless, though sympathetic? Is there even the chilling possibility that the Gnostics are right and God is not good? Heaven forbid! I am reminded of the encounter between the Samaritan woman and Jesus: *"Sir," the woman said, "You have nothing to draw with and the well is deep..." (John 4:11).* Indeed, this well is deep and I feel totally ill-equipped to draw the truth of God out of this. Nevertheless, left to my own devices, I press on in the true spirit of a jackleg preacher.

Recall how the apostles were so disturbed by Jesus' restful repose in the midst of a storm that they asked the question, *"Teacher, don't you care if we drown?"* (Mark 4:38). They called to him because he was sacked out so calmly on a cushion in the middle of a violent storm. I was reminded of this once when I found myself in the middle of a personal storm and was unable to go to church for the worship service and a special program. The person responsible for the program confronted me some days later to let me know his displeasure with me for missing the program. His question was quick and direct, "Don't you care...?" He did not inquire about my health; he did not pray for me or express any concern about why I had missed the event. He simply hurled the question that Jesus heard from the disciples.

When millions died in various disasters, distressed believers cried out, "God, don't you care?" God's apparent inaction led some to say that God was sleeping, others that he must be dead, and others that he must not care. The best defense from some of the faithful was a wishy-washy, "He cares but is powerless to act." Or we throw up our hands, quote Isaiah, and call it a day. *"For my thoughts are not your thoughts, neither are your ways my ways," declares the Lord. "As the heavens are higher than the earth, so are my ways higher than your ways and my thoughts than your thoughts."* (Isaiah 55:8-9).

There is a hidden implication in the invocation of that scripture that we sinful human beings would have acted when God did not. The charge against God cannot be ignored. The righteousness of the stance we believe we would have taken is confronted by the apparent failure of God to get involved. What we mean is, "I don't have a clue what God is doing but if I were God..." And then we stop. The chill of our nearly blasphemous impertinence shocks us into a new period of mute resignation.

I found a clue about how to think about this unsettling subject as I was writing chapter 5 on the "Theology of the Small." Jesus may have used his persistent talk about God who is "near", God "within", God "in our midst" to try to help us to understand how God's Spirit operates. We are so focused on what we can see that we lose sight of what can be perceived from the non-visual. We need to look anew at creation. There are some abilities that are inherent in us that can effect miraculous changes. God expects us, the human faithful, to invoke these features for the good of the people of God.

This well is deep. It is so deep in fact that I found myself moving away from the normal inadequate words of prose and trying to draw from this well with a bucket of poetic expressions in my poem entitled, *The Inside God.*

where was God
in the holocaust?
in the middle passage
with millions lost?
when you keep on losing
and cannot win
is that when God
is hiding in?
way down in my soul
working to make me whole
and rescue me
from temptation round
all of us down
on the ground
does God in me
know God in you?
does God know God
in others too?
is God in all
or just one sect
the specially chosen
the divine elect
do evil people
have a spark
of God residing
in their heart
I know my God
resides within
because sometimes I feel
something akin
to love
or at least
a good feeling
toward my human peer
and not just when
I'm kneeling
at the altar

with them near
a good feeling
that replaces the fear
I naturally feel
when someone's feet
come near my heels
and remind me that my space
is invaded and defaced
by someone not my
gender or race or size
someone whose eyes
have seen other horizons
God within makes me accept
despite the feelings
long kept buried
in my subconscious brain
the "excuse me"
proffered tentatively
by a member of
the human domain
who no longer seems
so low and mean
the God within me urges
your God inside
to act in concert
to override
the malevolent surges
to change the courses
of history
from bad desires
to goodness
from base and low
to movement higher
from wishes to malign
to benevolent designs
but when does God
within come out

when do we push
aside the doubt
that causes us to hesitate
when we should try to relate
the godliness that sets forth
the other's value and worth
when God inside
joins forces with others
with God inside
together they further
the cause of good
now turned
inside out
the inside God
is heard to shout
unification
combination
something within
then
you, me, us
together
an act of God
the holocaust ended
when all the inside Gods
turned out
to marshal their forces and
turn the troops about
slavery stopped
or paused at least
when together minds
rushed to the fore
and stayed this beast
crying, "enough, no more!"
and slammed the door
God is within
alive, not dead
but stifled by the need

to get ahead
that silences each
dissenting voice
forcing good
to give the choice
to evil actors
of unchecked play
that lets the demons
have their way
in other words
the human resistance
to getting involved
and providing assistance
But only through
Joining the God in you
Can my inside God
Have life, too

That's it! God is not silent or uncaring and certainly not malevolent. God is in our midst; God is in us. God in me combines with God's presence in you so that we become God's agents and instruments for change. Over the years many theologians have proposed this simple idea. God condemned the holocaust through us when we exorcised the demons of silence and found our voices of protest. Howard Thurman, a great theologian of the last century, wrote about how the God within one species can communicate with the God within another to bring about the possibility of peaceful interaction when he described the potentially lethal encounter between a child and a venomous snake. It reminds us that sometimes when it appears that God is silent or inactive or even disinterested, God is very active in the realm of the small kingdom within, urging us to manifest the divine intent in the world of the LARGE.

Sometimes the macroscopic manifestation of

God's influence comes in a way that masks the efficacy of God's action. For example, many believers were martyred before the collective influence of the kingdom within caused groups of individuals to rise in protest and overcome the enemy. Dysgenic designs of dictators led to the murder of millions of innocent people before the kingdoms within marshaled their forces to end the pogrom. God was always involved and acting on behalf of the oppressed through the inner realm.

This leaves one remaining problem. This somewhat esoteric explanation for God's action through spiritual collaborations might work just fine for a corporate body, but what about the suffering individual? Does not God still appear to be uninvolved in that person's life? For me, the answer is that the Spirit of God within can and does heal the individual. That Spirit can direct molecular actors to alter their behavior and change malignant cells to benign.

He said, "If you listen carefully to the voice of the LORD your God and do what is right in his eyes, if you pay attention to his commands and keep all his decrees, I will not bring on you any of the diseases I brought on the Egyptians, for I am the LORD, who heals you." (Exodus 15:26). God *forgives all your sins and heals all your diseases, (Psalm 103:3). Jesus went throughout Galilee, teaching in their synagogues, preaching the good news of the kingdom, and healing every disease and sickness among the people. (Matthew 4:23).* However, if physical healing or relief is not in God's plan, the inner presence of the Holy Spirit still provides precious comfort during times of pain and stress.

Epilogue

THIS IS MY STORY
And I'm Sticking to It

Each of you is to take up a stone on his shoulder, according to the number of the tribes of the Israelites, to serve as a sign among you. In the future, when your children ask you 'What do these stones mean?' tell them that the flow of the Jordan was cut off before the arch of the covenant of the Lord when it crossed the Jordan, the waters of the Jordan were cut off. These stones are to be a memorial to the people of Israel forever." (Joshua 4:5-7).

I wrote this book because I believe that we must take seriously the questions and unspoken concerns of people who are not formally trained theologians but who are thinking about God nevertheless. They intuitively know and love God but cannot reconcile the image of God as love with some preachers' insistent cry for eternal torture and vengeance. I write to give people permission to ask the questions that fear of God's wrath precluded in the past.

Furthermore, I wanted to prod those who have painted the pictures of God to consider that God may have been serious when warnings were written giving proscriptions against images. Moreover, God has always been mindful of both genders and every ethnic group and race. The historical record shows very clearly the African participation in the development of the early Christian church. You can't really avoid it unless you put blinders over your mental eyes and your intellect. God even decreed that an African would be the one to

150

help a brutally beaten Jesus bear the cross during the last agonizing stage of his journey to the crucifixion site. *Luke* records it this way: *"and as they led him away, they seized Simon from Cyrene who was on his way in from the country and put the cross on him and made him bear it behind Jesus."* (Luke 23:26).

A religion with such an ordained African presence is a religion that is inclusive. Everyone--not just Europeans and Africans--has a part in this story. That's why we have to take the opportunity to say to the world that this is our story and we're sticking to it! While on others God was calling, God did not pass anyone by. It is recorded in God's holy word that we were present, involved and in the mind of God.

Some would argue that my obsession with the race question and the whitewashing of God is merely a reflection of my own racism. That may be so. But I suggest that even I have a nobler intent. No one can worship the true God if he or she insists on worshiping the American idol or some other god of their creation. No one can see God and be truly born again if he or she remains fixated on the images created by Michelangelo or Leonardo da Vinci. Even white men cannot be saved by the white man's idol god. My plea is that all of us, like Simon Peter, must repent and return to God through Jesus Christ so that we can strengthen our brothers and sisters.

Spectacular events like falling Jericho walls, Jesus walking on water, and Jesus and the disciples feeding the multitude all were miraculous but not necessarily supernatural. The God who created nature does not need to transcend nature when it is possible to transform human hearts.

The strange chapter about the Theology of the Small forces us to consider the deep and unsettling idea that God operates and makes divine decisions in all dimensions including the realm of the small. The quantum is as much in the domain of God as the tornado. Sometimes, macroscopic manifestations come from the cumulative effect of decisions at the microscopic level. A massive hurricane with all of its destructive power is the energized collection of tiny molecules of oxygen, nitrogen and water.

I sum it all up with something the great jackleg theologians among my ancestors said. They would express their ideas about God the only way that they could without causing alarm in the big house. They would sing a song. You know the song. *I got shoes, you got shoes, all God's chill'un got shoes.* In other words, my brothers and my sisters, *all* God's children--the emphasis is on *all*--have a part in God's kingdom! This is my story and I'm sticking to it!

www.ingramcontent.com/pod-product-compliance
Lightning Source LLC
Chambersburg PA
CBHW031513040426
42445CB00009B/206